Single *and* Content

Experiencing Singleness
in a Paired-Off World

Dana Anders,
Nathan Clement,
Chris Conti,
and Lana Trent

WORD PUBLISHING
NASHVILLE
A Thomas Nelson Company

Word Publishing
Single and Content
Copyright © 1999 by Dana Anders, Nathan Clement, Chris Conti, Lana Trent

Unless otherwise indicated, all Scripture references are taken from the New International Version ®. NIV ®. Copyright © 1973, 1978, 1984 by International Bible Society. Used by permission of Zondervan Publishing House.

References marked NASB are from the New American Standard Bible, © 1960, 1962, 1963, 1968, 1971, 1975, 1977 by The Lockman Foundation. Used by permission.

References marked KJV are taken from the King James Version.

Because of the sensitive nature of personal stories in this book, some of the names have been changed.

ISBN 0-8499-3719-1

Printed in the United States of America
99 01 02/ QPV / 4 3 2 1

Contents

Acknowledgments   V

Introduction   VII

1: From the Freezer to the Microwave in the Same Box   1

(Lifestyle)

    Staying Single Longer   2

    To Rent or to Own   6

    The Great Roommate Debate   11

    Roommate Stories   21

    Pets and That Added Responsibility   27

    Neat Freak or Slob?   31

    Eating Habits   37

    The Fight against Flab   44

    Someone to Hang With   48

    The Need for Accountability   55

2: God Gave All of Us Twenty-Four Hours in the Day   60

(Work and Ministry)

    Affording Good Money Decisions   61

    Insuring Yourself   67

    Working Hard for the Money   71

    Time Management   78

    Vacations   84

    Off the Clock   89

    Serving in Church   93

    Ministry   97

3: Not Yet Promoted to the Grown-Up Table   102

(Awkward Situations)

Family Expectations   103

When a Friend Gets Married   111

I'll Never Do That at My Wedding   117

Holiday Hoopla Can Hurt   120

Going to Reunions   126

Feeling Puny and Wanting Mommy   130

4: Looking for the Holy Grail Woman—or Man   136

(Dating)

The Media's Impact on Dating   136

Dating and the Christian Perspective   144

Do I Have Only One, One and Only?   155

Who Asks? Who Pays?   161

The Perfect Date   166

The Unusual, the Embarrassing, and the Unexpected   170

Staying Pure   175

Having the "We-Gotta-Talk" Talk   185

Recovering from a Broken Relationship   189

5: You Can't Waller in It   195

(Contentment)

Becoming Content   195

Opening the Gift of Singleness   207

Struggling with Loneliness   213

The Waiting Room   221

The Other Voices   229

Survey Information   237

Notes   239

About the Authors   241

Acknowledgments

The authors would like to offer a few words of thanks.

To our interviewees: Thank you for being so generous with your time and for being so honest and candid as we talked.

To the management companies or staff of our interviewees: Thanks for working with us.

To our team at Word Publishing: Bethany Bothman, Valerie Bower, Lee Gessner, Tim LaDeau, Ami McConnell, Jana Muntsinger, Jennifer Stair, and others. Thanks for believing in us!

To those who completed our survey: Thanks for sharing your thoughts.

To our family and friends: Thanks for supporting us.

To Jodi Bloss: Thanks for being our alternate interview team member.

And to Midge Trent, Lana's mom, and others who helped us enter survey data: Thanks for all your help.

Introduction

Single and content: these two words seem to be an oxymoron. But God has called us to be content no matter our circumstances, so we are working on being content in our singleness. Writing this book has caused us to evaluate our feelings and refocus on God's plan, and we hope it will do the same for you.

We want to encourage you, challenge you, make you laugh, and, most of all, show you that you are not alone in your singleness. Did you know that 45 percent of the adults in the United States are single right now?

In this book, you will hear the voices of four Christian singles, be encouraged by more than twenty never-married Christian music artists and others who minister to singles, and gain perspective from our survey of 555 singles who know where you are.

This is not intended to be a self-help or "how-to-find-a-mate" book. Our intent is for you, the Christian single, to be encouraged by other Christian singles. Although you may feel completely alone in your singleness, you will encounter many other singles who are struggling with these same issues. We hope that you will see yourself in the stories shared by both well-known and "average Joe" singles and, like each of us, begin to discover the secret of being content in your singleness.

So when does a person actually become "single"? We are all single at birth, as recording artist Mitch McVicker said, but the realization of our single status hits each of us at some point. For the four of us, after we graduated from college and moved into our first apartment, it began to hit home that we were single.

For others, the realization could be more abrupt: "Thirty hurt me. When I turned thirty, it was like, 'Wow. I'm out of clean clothes. I gotta get married,'" said Geof Barkley, Christian music artist and former member of Geoff Moore & The Distance.

Or it could take someone else to point it out: "Up until I was twenty-three or twenty-four, my parents were always like, 'You're too young to date' or 'Why are you dating so seriously? Don't get tied down.' Then, all of a sudden, I passed a magic point where yesterday I wasn't old enough to date, then today my parents are wondering what I did to make that nice girl from Canada go away. Then I thought, *Oh my gosh, my parents think I need to be dating. I've reached a brand new level of low,*" said Max Hsu from Church of Rhythm.

Our challenge (and yours) is to stop seeing ourselves as singles and start seeing ourselves as God does.

Rich Mullins, former singer and songwriter, offered a good perspective on this issue: "If people identify themselves as being single or married they are probably misidentifying themselves. It's sort of like identifying yourself as being one race or another. I generally think most of us are something other than, or at least beyond, the sum of our strengths, weaknesses, genes, environment—all those things."

1

From the Freezer to the Microwave in the Same Box
(Lifestyle)

Dumping my day's cargo in the living room, I change into my comfy, home clothes and nibble on fat-free potato chips as I nuke a frozen entrée. Flipping on the TV, I sit back and let the remote do the walking.

The gym bag I packed three days ago sits there on the floor taunting me, as does that exercise equipment I bought in a weak, yet optimistic, moment from a 2:00 A.M. infomercial.

The microwave beeping reminds me that dinner is served and that the evening has just begun. I have a meeting at church and a few calls to return.

A partially solid glass of milk sits in the sink. Rolling my eyes at my roommate's insensitivity, I rinse it and put it in the dishwasher.

With pen in hand, I dial our voice service, burning my tongue on the veal parmesan.

Beep. I have a call from Julie, who wants me to do some lay-out work for her. I'm not really excited about doing it, but who else will do it if I don't? I leave a message on her machine to fax me the details.

Beep. Scott says that we need another person for volleyball on Saturday. I make a note to call Mike and Bill.

Beep. Mom called. She says that my nephew asked, in his two-year-old voice, if I could come over. I chuckle at the phrase "come over" because it's not easy to do two hundred miles away. My chuckle gives way to conviction. Should I be spending more time with my family? Mom mentions, in the way only a mom can, that she hasn't heard from me in a while and asks the "social butterfly" to return her call.

Oh yeah, I'm the social butterfly, but I'm the roommate without a date this weekend. . . . Wait a minute, or this month!

Staring at the calendar as I eat my dinner, now cool, I plot out my week.

I need to take my car in for an oil change. I keep putting it off, but horror stories of roommates having to replace engines make me put it on my day planner for Thursday.

I take another bite of my green beans.

Looking at my reflection in the patio window, I realize how much my life is like this frozen dinner, as if life could be put into little compartments. It represents my attempt to be healthy while hurried and my attempt to balance work and play, God's plan and mine, what others want of me and what I can give.

Okay. So the cherry cobbler dessert was gone first. Can I help it?

Staying Single Longer
"Why spoil the relationship by getting married?"

Chris—It could be a good thing that more people are waiting to marry. We can only hope that they are thinking more about their decisions and not making as many wrong choices. However, statistics don't favor that idea, as divorce rates among non-Christians and Christians continue to rise. My guess is that more people are choosing to live together and either don't care to "enter that institution" or say, "Why spoil a perfectly good relationship by getting married?"

Why am I still waiting? Some say that my standards are too high. My brothers say that I'm expecting a perfect guy and a "Brady Bunch" family. Maybe I watch too much TV, or maybe I want to rely on God to give me this desire of my heart.

MY ADVICE TO YOU IS TO GET MARRIED: IF YOU FIND A GOOD WIFE YOU'LL BE HAPPY; IF NOT, YOU'LL BECOME A PHILOSOPHER.
—SOCRATES

I want a family that sits down for meals and turns off the TV as they talk over the day. A family that touches, says, "I love you," communicates with each other, and builds a ministry together.

And should this be my destiny, I'm willing to wait.

Lana—I certainly thought I'd be married by now. Am I choosing to stay single longer? I would say "no." I'm not choosing to be single. No one has asked me to marry him. A seven-year-old boy once told me that if I wore more makeup, it would help. Regardless, I've been in love, and others have been in love with me. So far, it just hasn't happened at the same time where we knew it was right. Why are people in general staying single longer? I think it's harder to meet people than it used to be, and people are more focused on their careers.

Dana—I may only be five years out of college, but to me, that's five years more of singleness than I expected. I'm trying to concentrate on the other things that God has for me. Being single is normal to me—for now. Many people like me seem to be concentrating on their careers and enjoying having his or her own schedule. I don't think I am staying single by choice, but I am more open to the single idea, as long as I keep my focus.

The longer I am single, the more particular I have become about the company I choose. At this point, I'd rather be single than date the wrong guy. But the question is: How do I know who the wrong guy is? Right now, I am trying to make it easier on myself, not focusing on dating relationships. I have been praying for friendships with fun, Christian males, and, if something comes from a friendship, then the Lord would have my attention. Meanwhile, I prefer to look the other direction.

Nathan—I really believe that people are simply afraid of getting divorced. The divorce rate has served as a pretty good deterrent to marriage lately. I heard there's an idea of establishing a marriage covenant law to accompany the existing law we have for marriage. This law would make it very difficult for couples to divorce. It is based upon scriptural reasons for divorce instead of granting "no-fault" divorces. I think Christians should be in favor of this and, if it is passed, be signing on the dotted line. If millions of young Christians committed to this kind of marriage, we would send a strong message to the rest of the world about what we think of this institution. It would also make us consider our decision as soundly as we ought to, knowing we couldn't get out of the marriage simply because "the flame has gone out."

I think another reason is that people just don't believe marriage is necessary anymore. The generally accepted idea is that if two people love each other and are living together, then that's all they need.

People also see that there is so much living to be done before they get married. Not that marriage ends all the fun, but there is a modicum of freedom that singles enjoy: not having to be accountable to another for the money, being able to travel, the opportunity to meet a lot of people before we settle down.

Other Voices

Max Hsu, Church of Rhythm—This generation wants to change the world. Our parents' generation came out of a war culture, and they really value things like stability and security, which they didn't have growing up. But we've had it and take it for granted. So we're into things like creative expression and changing the world. All my friends want to save the planet.

[Singleness is] more culturally acceptable. It used to be: "Here's your path: You go to high school. You go to college. You get married. You have babies and a house with a white picket fence." But many people aren't satisfied with that. They are reacting to that, and they say, "I'm myself, and I'm going to find something unique and different to do." I think it is also a healthier generation coming up. We're a lot more aware of the issues and breaking patterns like codependency and that kind of thing. I think we've been waiting to grow up some.

Grover Levy—I think people in my generation are staying single longer because we're more distrustful of the institution of marriage. So many of our parents had failed marriages. Our generation realizes that forever is a long time, and we want to make the right decision. Another part of it is that our generation is the first in a long time whose earning power is less than its parents', and many of us, although we've gone to college, are having a hard time making enough money to support a family.

Nee-C Walls, Anointed—I hope people are staying single longer because we really want what God wants for us, and we really want His will to be done. A lot of us Christians have been hurt from dating and being in relationships, and we are scared. Some of us are scared to hook up with people, and some of us are really anxious. *God is like, "I'll wait till you calm down so you won't get yourself all caught up in something that you can't get yourself out of."*

Heather Floyd, Point of Grace—People's priorities have changed. Some may not even care about marriage because they are so career-minded. When my mom was younger, her goal was to get married and have a family. It's not like that nowadays. First they get their career started, then they may start looking.

Pam Thum—Sometimes people don't want to commit. Many haven't seen a whole lot of shining examples of laughter and joy and passion and friendship. I would say very few marriages demonstrate the love of Jesus to the Church.

To Rent or to Own
"I'll just buy my own stinkin' white picket fence."

Nathan—I think that I realized I was single when I signed my first lease. It was one of the first adult things that I did on my own. At first, I was excited, but it wasn't long before the excitement parted way for a mild wave of dread that pushed through. This was it. I was beginning my single life.

When the big day came, it didn't take long to move in. My family helped, and it was all over in a few hours. The rest of the day was spent deciding where I would put each item of *my* stuff in *my* place. I was giving orders. It felt good. It was my hallway, my bathroom, my living room, my dining room, my kitchen, my back door, and my neighbors. But then the evening came, and everyone hugged and left. And it was a pause in my whole life.

It turned out to be not so bad. I put things away, flicked on the TV but didn't sit down, and worked until I fell into my bed (okay, my mattress on the floor) exhausted. The next morning was exciting, not lonely, and I soon fell into my routine. I have rented for eight years and have relished my time alone. I have learned to take care of my own stuff—how to yell at landlords, how to recognize a phone solicitation before the caller even speaks, how to get lime off of my glassware, and how to avoid getting locked out of my apartment or car.

I think buying a house is a signal that you are now settled in whatever state you find yourself and are ready for the long haul. If you're single and buy a house, it says, "This is probably the way it's going to be for a long time, and I'm ready for it"—which, I think, is a good thing. To be able to accept your single-ness and invest in a location like that, I believe, allows you to start focusing on important things like getting involved in church, putting down roots to establish long-term friendships, and sticking with the career you're in. At some point, even though we believe that we have the advantage of being "foot-loose and fancy free" and can jump around the country when-ever we want, we need to get settled and familiar with the landscape.

I just turned thirty-two, and I'm beginning to reach that point that I feel I need to be in a house. I'm not fresh out of college anymore, and it seems like I should be maximizing my buck by owning something. There are a couple of old factories con-verted to condos; they are offering low down payments to people who want to refurbish old homes downtown. Maybe I should get a Realtor.

Chris—I currently live with two other Christian women in a large A-frame house that we rent. I think I'll rent until I marry. I used to think that if a woman buys a house it was kind of like saying, "I'm okay with being single forever. Don't worry about me. I can do it all alone." It was almost like giving up. Now I see that buying a house is a sound investment, but with a teacher's salary, I don't see a down payment in the near future.

555 Singles Surveyed

On the Topic of Living Arrangements

Rent   68%
Own   20%
Live with
Parents   12%

Dana—Right now I share an apartment on the northeast side of Indianapolis with my roommate, Susan. I've rented here for almost four years, as this marks my place of independent living after completing "the five-year plan" at Indiana University. Prior to Susan joining me, my friend Jenny and I shared the place until Jenny felt it was time to pursue owning her own home. After many months of research, meetings with the Realtor, and enduring the tedious closing process, Jenny moved out into a distinct area of the city where many young professionals reside.

Owning a home sounds exciting, but I don't think I'm quite up to taking that huge step alone. Like many others, I have always assumed that the first house I would live in would be the one I shared with my husband. We could have home-cooked meals in our dining room and decorate and maintain our place together. I suppose that would be possible with a female roommate who could also contribute to the mortgage payments, but I would still prefer having that first home with my husband. Even though I might be throwing away a lot of money on rent,

I do see some advantages for this time in my life. I like that I don't have to fix the leaky faucet, replace the old furnace, repaint the walls, or mow the lawn. The maintenance man has become my friend. And I definitely enjoy the swimming pool available to apartment residents during the muggy summer months.

Lana—At this point in my life, a lot of people are telling me that I should buy a house. I have a good job and have begun to save, but it's so much responsibility! Right now, I rent. I pay very little, and when big things break, the landlord has to pay for the repair. I like that. I don't have to find three hundred dollars for the plumber. Recently, the city of Indianapolis decided that our street needed to be on a sewer line. The bill to my landlord was over eight thousand dollars, and he didn't have a choice. Renting isn't too bad. However, I also don't like the idea of throwing money away on rent. Maybe in the next few years I'll buy a house, but I'd also really like to have a husband to help make this monumental purchase.

Other Voices

Heather Floyd, Point of Grace—I rent a condo right now. I'm in the process of thinking about buying something. This is that old-fashioned mind-set. Every girl thinks, I don't want to buy a house because someday my husband and I will buy one together. A great book Lady in Waiting *talks about how girls put things off till "the day": I'll do this when I meet this guy or when I'm married. Then you're fifteen years down the road and you haven't bought a house or started investing, where if you had you'd be so much better off. If you buy now then marry, you can just find someplace else. It's not that I'm waiting that much, but to do it on my own is scary to me. I want my dad to go, "So, honey, here's what you do."*

9

I want someone to do it all for me. I don't know anything about the financial part. My manager and Realtor just told me that they will help me with that. I get a paper every Sunday and I look through all the homes. I do think about it, but I think God will give me the desire to buy a home when the time comes. And He has just planted the thought for now. I don't have the motivation yet. I'm embarking on thinking about it.

Larry Burkett, Christian Financial Concepts—In general, buying is better than renting, since you can't gain equity through renting. Owning a home is a practical decision for many single adults. Singles usually have fewer household expenses than families with children and can save more for down payments and pay more into equities. Then if a single marries, the equity can be transferred to a larger home. Those who remain single will still need a debt-free home in their older years.

Rebecca St. James—It would be really hard for me to move out of my parents' home. I know it's gonna happen someday. In the near future it would be hard because I rely on my family so much. But, in a way, I almost feel that it would be good for me to be lonely. If I experience that, when I do get married I will appreciate my husband so much more than if I hadn't experienced the loneliness. So in marriage when I'm feeling crowded or wanting a little bit more time alone, I'll remember those times of loneliness and be so glad that I have him.

Nee-C Walls, Anointed—I love it by myself. I really do. Right before I moved I got that feeling in my heart, "I've got to move; I've got to get out of here." I went out and started buying furniture by faith. I didn't know where I was gonna live. I started buying stuff in advance.

The Great Roommate Debate
"I like my stuff the way it is."

Dana—Roommates are a good thing, even a great thing. I thought that being single would mean claiming successful independence, needing no one, toughing it out on your own. But it seems more and more singles like sharing their dwelling place with their friends and having company and companionship, whether it's in a house or an apartment. Personally, I'd probably go crazy without someone to talk to after enduring the daily grind. Just knowing my roommate is home gives me a sense of comfort and security, whether we actually have a quality conversation every day or not.

Susan, my current roommate, is the best; I can't believe how well we get along. It seems our best conversations are after 11:00 at night and around 10:00 on lazy Saturday mornings. Some discussions are serious, and others simply happen because we feel like talking a long time about random things that make us laugh. I think healthy roommate situations are crucial. I have been friends with all of my past roommates, but it seems as though Susan and I have a friendship that carries over into a healthy roommate relationship.

Susan is one of the most organized gals I know. Her tendencies go beyond house cleaning to monthly storage closet or food pantry maintenance to sock drawer coordination. Her room has an eclectic, stylish feel and is never cluttered. She's decorated and organized our place with every effort to create that homey, personalized feeling. She has a knack for making the simplest thing look like an amazing piece of artwork.

On a few occasions, I've returned home and heard "Spring" from Vivaldi's *The Four Seasons* through the front door, then entered to breathe in the familiar aroma of fresh paint. I've begun to associate hearing that music with something being painted, arranged, or decorated. I never know what to expect; it is quite comical. I love her tastes in décor—that is not even an issue—the surprise factor is what makes everything so interesting. Once our dining room changed color and texture for a good two weeks . . . the finished product, beautiful.

> ### A Few Reasons Why Having a Roommate Can Be Handy
>
> 1. There is someone to blame if the answering machine is left off.
> 2. Moving furniture takes less ingenuity.
> 3. You don't have to feel left out when fast-food restaurants run two-for-one dinner specials.
> 4. You don't have to assume all house noises are prowlers.
> 5. Your Christmas tree has more presents.
> 6. You have someone to help if the refrigerator falls on you.
> 7. You spend less time wondering how long it will take for your body to be found if you die suddenly.
>
> Taken from Michael Nolan and Eve Sarrett, *I'm So Tired of Other People, I'm Dating Myself* (Nashville, Tenn.: Thomas Nelson Publishers, 1993).

We have shared odd jobs around the place, like rotating dishwasher duty, but she actually offers to haul the trash and vacuum—I do other things, so everything works out. Our shared living space is always kept neat and clean—even with the cats, Molly and Mufasa. Susan is very responsible for her "babies" and makes it a point to stay on shedding patrol. Though I have never been a big fan of cats, I learned right away what was most important to consider—having a good roommate. After interviewing me, the felines insisted that they would only enhance, not hinder, my rooming with Susan.

Lana—I lived by myself once. I hated it. It was horrible, and I could only do it for one month. I still refer to that apartment with a pet name that is not repeatable.

Roommates can be great, and I prefer having more than just one. It takes more than one to handle my extroversion. Some of my best friends have been my roommates; however, some of my friendships have also been severely strained by living together.

Having a roommate is a lot like marriage or a family relationship. It can be wonderful or a nightmare. My first roommate was my sister. I don't remember having a choice in the matter, and I can't say I remember the arrangement very fondly. She is two years older than I, and being older gave her the power position in our roommate relationship. But even this family example illustrates one of the best reasons for having a roommate: economics. With four kids, my parents couldn't afford a five-bedroom home.

There are definitely financial benefits to having a roommate. However, I am an advocate for roommates even when you can afford to live on your own. Presently, I live in a three-bedroom A-frame that I share with two others. We have a great place. I couldn't live on my own for the same amount without giving up a lot.

In college, nine of us rented a house. I paid four hundred dollars for rent for the entire year! Of course, with extra people come more opportunities for conflict.

I also appreciate the benefit of not having to buy everything to make my place complete. Presently, I provide mainly the toys in our house: the stereo, TV, and PC. My roommates provide the furniture. By combining my assets with others, I get the benefit of a complete place without going into incredible debt or living without. On the downside, I am sharing my stuff.

Roommates provide me with companionship. Research shows that people who live alone have a higher rate of depression and suicide. Living alone creates a greater risk of emotional and mental difficulties. However, there are many healthy, well-adjusted people who have a good support system and do well on their own.

And if you can afford to live on your own, our society thinks you should. I see this in two popular TV sitcoms: *Friends* and *Seinfeld.* Having a roommate in your twenties, like in *Friends,* is viewed as necessary for economic reasons. But if you're over thirty, as in *Seinfeld,* and living with someone of the same sex, people often assume that you're involved in an alternative lifestyle. This annoys me.

I feel safer having a roommate, someone to turn on the front porch light. If I don't come home one night, one of my roommates will notice. If I lived alone, it might take a while.

Sometimes I need accountability to keep me in tow. For example, I am a software addict and sometimes tend to be a slob. I am neater having a roommate. My bedroom might be a disaster (and it often is), but at least the common areas are picked up. Also, my roommates usually notice when I have come home from a shopping spree. And if they know I'm struggling financially, I'm less likely to buy.

I am not saying that roommates should be surrogate parents, however. All of us have weak areas in our lives. Anyone who has been on a diet or tried to stop an ingrained habit knows that there is indeed strength in numbers. Having someone holding us accountable really helps.

I've been told roommates are a great preparation for marriage because you learn how to live with someone who was raised differently and may have contrary ideas of how things should be done. If this is true, and, considering I have had more than thirty roommates, I often ask God if I'm not yet ready.

I admit that there are disadvantages to sharing a residence: You have to compromise. You don't have as much privacy. You are taking a risk and can experience personality and other types of conflicts. If you choose the right person and act responsibly, though, you may not experience these disadvantages.

Probably the most important thing to me about my roommates is that they are my friends and, often, a surrogate family. They are my sisters. Some people don't think it's necessary to be friends with their roommates. One of my past roommates never verbalized it, but that's how she lived. She would come home, and I would say, "How are you?" She would respond, "Fine," and that was it. In the five months I lived with her, she never asked me how I was.

When I lived in college with the nine girls, I learned one valuable lesson for helping people get along. We organized the house to minimize conflict. The more up-front "rules" and expectations there were, the better we got along. I'm a big believer in this and continue to live by this today. By having very clear expectations, we minimize the feeling of martyrdom and bitterness when someone doesn't do her share. At our house, we have house jobs. We each have our own voice mailbox, and our phone bill comes already divided. We also have a house checking account.

I have learned a lot about myself by having so many different roommates. For example, I've learned that I am more sensitive to sound than light. Roommate #23 and I shared a room, and she was sensitive to light. This didn't work out too well, since I got up early and turned on the light, and she'd stay up late and make a lot of noise.

I've also been educated about personality types, spiritual gifts, and temperaments. For example, I would prefer not to live with those with the spiritual gift of prophecy. "Prophets" love to discern truth and point out faults in others. I personally like to ignore my faults as much as I can. I like having structure and organization. I have my CDs in alphabetical order, and, for some, that might be more than they can handle. It is for this reason that I always try to spend time with a roommate prospect before she moves in. We had one roommate prospect who was so thorough in checking us out that she did a "test sleep-over."

Confrontation, communication, and compromise are very important things to consider in roommate relationships or any type of relationship. It's always a challenge to know when I should accept someone's little irritating habits or when I should say something. (Why is it that no one in our house ever puts their dirty dishes in the dishwasher? Does it take that much more effort to open the door and insert the dish than to put the dish in the sink?)

When there is a conflict, it's important to say something before it becomes a big deal. I've learned I can't sweat the small stuff. I need to be approachable, open-minded, and willing to laugh at myself.

555 Singles Surveyed

On the Subject of Having Roommates

Do   49%
Don't 41%

Chris—I prefer to live with people. I like to have someone to share my experiences with, to talk with while I brush my teeth. I like the financial benefits, of course. But, most of all, I'm scared to death to live alone.

When I started teaching, I lived in an unfurnished apartment—my first time ever not to have a roommate. With six kids in my family, I never before experienced silence (or easy access to the bathroom or phone). I'd hear strange noises and wonder if someone was breaking in to kill me on a Friday night and if anyone would notice until Monday when I didn't show up for first period.

I'm what you would call a "scaredy cat." Recently, I made the mistake of seeing the movie *Kiss the Girls*. I have never been so affected by a movie. Afterward, I was afraid to walk out to my car in the dark. When I got up enough nerve, I'd sprint, open the door, and—in one motion—sit down, throw my bags in the back, and lock the door. Then I'd sigh, though my heart would be pounding.

I had nightmares. Every noise I heard, I thought of a corresponding scene in the movie. *I'm walking out to my car, and so was this girl when she was nabbed. That girl rolled over and looked at her alarm clock, and so did I.*

I wasn't comfortable anytime after dark alone in the house. I still won't take the trash out after dark either. One week, my roommate reminded me that it was my turn for trash detail, and I said, "I know." I knew full well, though, that I wasn't about to walk to the side of the house to get the cans then drag them to the street, making this screeching sound. She doesn't seem to understand my fear. The next week she made me go with her to take the trash out. There's safety in numbers, you know. The victims are always divided and conquered in movies.

Our neighborhood seems pretty safe, and apparently we have a security system too. Someone at a party once leaned up against a red button on the stairway, and the cops showed up. So, even though we aren't charged a monthly fee, we think we have some sort of emergency button.

But if an intruder did grab me in the driveway, would I be

able to open the screen door, find the right key, and unlock the door?

My only comfort during my week-long trauma was having my roommates at home. I could feel somewhat safe, though the thought of Lana taking on an intruder is quite funny.

Nathan—The next roommate I have will be a long-legged female who takes Sunday naps with me and shares the toothpaste. No, I haven't thrown in the towel and decided to shack up; I'm referring to marriage.

I know that roommates stave off the loneliness and help with rent and utilities, but I have chosen to go it alone. It's my space; it's my mess; or, at times, it's my inexplicable compulsive neatness. There's no one else around to fiddle with it. I can never figure out how people with roommates keep items in the refrigerator straight. I wouldn't want someone drinking my milk if he didn't pay for part of it. What do you do? Divide the refrigerator in half? Go shopping together and pool resources? Or just assume that it's all going to come out even in the end? When my college roommate and I loaned money to each other, we joked that we would have to have a Jewish Year of Jubilee (the year when all debts are wiped clean) instead of trying to sort it all out.

Other Voices

Janna Potter, Avalon—I'm going to buy a house, but right now I have a roommate in an apartment. It's like my roommate lives alone since I am gone so much. I've always roomed with friends who I knew so well I never had to wonder if we would get along.

Max Hsu, Church of Rhythm—We have a roommate who really believes in our ministry, so we have taken over the basement. We call it "the basement of testosterone." We moved in a year and a half ago and there's still no furniture here, but we have surround sound, laser disc, a pool table, a Ping-Pong table, snowmobiles, a punching bag, and an Olympic weight set. We're building a studio and we have all these guitars. And we've got more computers than I can count. So we have every boy toy on the planet and no furniture. Well, we have one couch.

I have my own room. When you get older, you dig that kind of thing. Like when you're in college, group living rocks, but when you get older, you're like, "I like my stuff the way it is."

We all sleep on the floor in sleeping bags. I now have a mattress. The mattress is a recent upgrade. We just don't have time. We're always upgrading the studio if we have time.

Michael Passons, Avalon—I like living by myself. I'm a real neat freak. I like to have control over my space. I used to live away from Nashville. No one would come to visit, so I moved back in town. I like having people around, but I want the option of not having them around. Best of both worlds.

Heather Floyd, Point of Grace—There are times I've been frustrated, but, when it boils down to it, I like living with people. I've thought about living alone, but my roommate now (for three years) is great. She even takes care of my dog. She even takes my dog home to her parents to visit.

I need a roommate. I prefer it. It's good for accountability too. She knows when I'm home and when I'm not.

Gary Mullet—I've gone through a billion roommates over the years—yeah, China was my roommate. And I just got to the point where I thought I would be a little happier by myself.

So the last three to four years I have lived by myself. And that's actually been nice. I think I've gotten to know who I am a little bit more. Right now I'm considering moving back in with some roommates, but I need a lot of space for my hobbies. The kitchen right now doubles as a shop. I've got a jigsaw sitting on the work counter and a workbench set up in there, because I never eat in there. I eat in front of the TV. If I move back in with other folks, I know I'm going to have to cut back on some of that. They might not like balsa dust all over the house.

Rich Mullins—There are three things that Beaker and I really concentrated on when we were living and working together and those are the three traditional monastic vows: the vow of obedience, the vow of poverty, and the vow of chastity. The goal of these three things are faith, hope, and love—that we live in awareness of faith, in awareness of hope, and in awareness of love.

So we worked that out for six to eight years—practicing, discovering—"When do I lean on you because I really need strength, and when do I lean on you just because I choose to be weak?" "When am I allowing you to use me to escape coming into a deeper experience with God, and when am I helping to direct you toward that experience?" "When is goofing off just a necessary part of having a full and rich life, and when does it become an obstacle to that?"

Pam Thum—Pick your roommates in the same way you would pick your friends. To me, your home is extremely important. It's almost like your heart: Guard it, for out of it are the issues of life. So, I don't think money should be a deciding factor for picking a roommate. To me, that is your home, and you've got to be really careful who you room with because if you're yoked, and I don't mean in marriage or in a boyfriend/girlfriend way, but if your values and what you believe are so diametrically opposed, then it's going to affect your entire life. I think you need to pick someone like you would a friend.

Benji Gaither, Benjamin—A good roommate is someone who doesn't smell, is fun, and is a spur-of-the-moment type.

Roommate Stories
"My crust is your crust."

Nathan—Single people have to do what they can to help each other when they are starting out. Rooming together is certainly one way to help cut expenses. The summer before my junior year, I moved into an apartment with two other guys. The place was run down and smelled stale. Our motto was: "It's only for three months." We survived by floating each other rent money, because we paid rent week by week, and sometimes one of us wouldn't have our paycheck yet. That's what friends do. The toughest thing, though, was food. Young guys like to eat. Loren discovered that you can buy four potpies for a buck and seemed to subsist on those for the whole summer. Once in a while we'd splurge. At the end of a long, hot summer workday, we would all come back to our stifling apartment and do what comes naturally to all college students: order pizza. I remember a few times when Loren just didn't have enough money and wouldn't let us treat him.

It would get so pitiful sometimes when the smell of the pizza would inevitably overwhelm him, and while we were eating, in mid-bite, he'd meekly ask, "Are you going to eat your crust?"

"Loren!" I'd say. "You can have a piece."

"No, no. I'll just have some crust, if you don't want it."

So, of course, being the good Christian that I am, I would give him a few scraps of bread.

Every time I think about this, I crack up. It's one of those impoverished college stories I'll never forget.

Chris—My first of eleven roommates in college was named "field mouse" by everyone on the floor because she was from a small town fifteen minutes away, and she shyly scampered down the hall to the restroom and back, or to class and back. She even cowered in the corner of our room, like I had a broom or something. Living with her, I learned the meaning of the term "painfully shy."

We rarely talked, although we were in the room together a lot. I tried to bring her into the group of friends I was making, but she would go home every weekend. Often she'd be packed on Thursday or she wouldn't unpack from the previous weekend. I think it hurt her that I was doing so well academically and socially, so I often wouldn't tell her about my day. Sometimes I'd hear her cry at night. Her face in her pillow, she tried to muffle the sobs, but I could hear her. It was a very uncomfortable situation. She left at midterm with a .6 GPA. We didn't stay in touch.

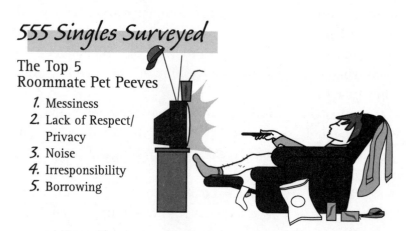

555 Singles Surveyed

The Top 5
Roommate Pet Peeves

1. Messiness
2. Lack of Respect/
   Privacy
3. Noise
4. Irresponsibility
5. Borrowing

Lana—I don't know what happens, but sometimes when two people become a couple, they change. Some type of personality osmosis occurs—all bets are off, and you don't know what to expect. This "couple disorder" affected one of my roommates one summer when I was in school. We lived in the Christian Campus House. Since our church sponsored it, there were definite guidelines in the house that we as residents agreed to abide by, and we signed a contract to do so. One of these rules was not to have men upstairs, in the bedroom area, after a certain time. My housemate was in love and was affected by this "couple disorder." I would wake up at 2:00 in the morning and hear her boyfriend in her room, or I'd be eating breakfast and see him come downstairs. I confronted them about it, but they didn't respond very well. They would tell me that they were only accountable to God and that I shouldn't judge them. It was an awful summer. Fortunately, it was only a summer. I'm not sure what I could have done differently, but I regret that, in the middle of the conflict, I lost their friendships.

Dana—I'd like to think of myself as a pretty easygoing roommate. As long as my roommate and I are able to compromise and don't let negative feelings stew until bursting, I am okay. Personal living space aside, I'm also kind of particular about our shared living areas. I don't think it's too much to ask to wipe food remnants off the kitchen stove or countertop. I like to keep pet hair off the sofa and definitely want a say in the temperature of the room. And as for guests, I most appreciate my roommates' boyfriends who keep a healthy perspective of time spent in our place and don't linger too late at night.

Have you ever known someone who was too nice? One of my roommates was from Germany and spoke little English. She was always giving a high-pitched greeting with a one-handed, quick, and happy wave. Didn't matter what time of the day it was, she would always stop, smile, and greet. She was so nice, but the word "overkill" somehow comes to mind. I wanted to be polite, but after a while, I didn't always feel like responding.

Some days she was lucky to get a pleasant nod out of me. I tried to be appreciative—at least she was consistent.

The hardest part about roommates, though, is figuring out how to read them. I can usually get along with anyone as long as I understand them. But the moody ones are so hard to figure out. One day they meet you at the breakfast table all chipper and chatty, completely interested in you and your life's happenings, and the next, they are agitated and silent—a wall would offer better conversation. One of my college roommates would swing on that pendulum. I never knew what to expect. But the good thing was, she knew she was moody, and it almost became a joke. I could tell by the way she walked down the hall whether I should acknowledge her or not. Some days, if I was brave and saw some hints of tolerance in her, I would smile and even snicker a bit and get right in her face with a bold, "Good morning, how's it going?" It was great, but it only worked because she knew she was difficult.

Other Voices

Jeff Frankenstein, Newsboys—*I had three days to drop out of college and join the Newsboys. So I had to find a place to live in Nashville, just a place to keep my stuff. Somehow my dad found someone he knew in Nashville who could put me up at his house. It was kind of weird. There was an apartment downstairs where this guy lived. Then upstairs there was a sixty-year-old lady. So we split the house three ways. She lived on one side of the house, and I lived on the other. She was really cool—a grandma-type lady. And I was really glad that she could put me up while I was trying to get adjusted. I was on the road a lot, and I'd come home a couple of days a week. One day she said, "I'm leaving to go on vacation, and I'll be back in a week or so," and she left.*

One morning I woke up and there were three cop cars in my

driveway. It was 6:00 in the morning, and they were beating on the door. Apparently she hadn't paid the rent in like two months. And I was sub-renting from her. So they handed me a warrant for her arrest. Two days later all our electricity was shut off. I put all my belongings in this room in the back corner of the house with a big note on the door saying, "Please don't repossess this. This is another guy's." Sure enough, two days later they came and repo-ed all the furniture and turned off the phone. And I was still living in the house. I lived there for three weeks in this empty house, and I had no furniture, sleeping on the floor. It was really weird.

Geof Barkley—I used to live with a guy who was a drummer, and his room was a picture of order and cleanliness. Outside of that, it was horrible. He never did the dishes. We went for a long time not doing them. And the dishes would pile up and pile up. The stuff that he cooked, he wouldn't even clean those. It got to a point where I would keep a fork and a knife and a plate and a glass in my room, and I would wash them when I got done using them and take them back up to my room.

Cherie Paliotta, Avalon—I have had horror stories. I have had roommates who have gotten into my business, causing lots of trouble. They stole my credit cards and my clothes and my shoes. Now I have the best roommate that I could ever ask for. We spiritually advise each other and encourage and lift each other up. We are sisters in the Lord, and that is the most important thing.

Max Hsu, Church of Rhythm—I think I was some people's worst roommate. I used to be really messy—a slob. I had this one roommate in college who was really neat and clean, and I wasn't. He got really frustrated with me because I just never *cleaned up, and one day he put all my stuff in a big trash can and left it in the middle of the room.*

Tips for Single Living

- Have a designated place where you and your single friends sit in church so that you will always have someone to sit with.

- Come up with a procedure for ensuring that you won't get locked out when you go out for a run. Keep an extra set of house keys in your shoes so you remember to take them with you.

- Buy appliances that turn themselves off.

- Face the coffee maker where you'll see it when you walk out the door. You won't forget to take your coffee with you, and you won't forget to turn the maker off.

- When solicitors call for the woman of the house, you can just say, "She's not home right now." Or move the phone away from your ear and yell, in your most childlike voice, "Mommmmmm, it's for you." Then let the phone sit there till they get the hint.

- When working late, call a friend and tell them that you'll call in twenty minutes when you get home, so they know that if they don't hear from you, you're in trouble.

- Make a party out of packing and moving. Supply food for people who help you move or fix something at your house. When moving, be packed and ready. Your moving friends will love you for it.

- Leave yourself voice mails for reminders.

- Cook on weekends and freeze portions separately for meals throughout the week.

- Even if you live alone, your recorded message on your answering machine should say, "We aren't home right now." Or get some burly guy to do the message. Or have two big dogs barking in the background.

- Exchange household duties with a friend of the opposite sex. Guys would mow your lawn if you would do their laundry.

- Stand over the sink when you eat so it's easy to clean.

Greg Long—Three or four of us were in the band house and the oldest, most responsible one—moi—got the phone in his name. For the most part, this was not a problem, but one day I came home and on the bill there were fifty dollars' worth of calls to 900 numbers. I was like, "We've got a problem. Who made the 900 number calls?" Of course, nobody made them. Some invisible man came in and dialed up the 900 numbers on my phone, so I ended up paying for them. After that, I restricted 900 numbers.

Jody McBrayer, Avalon—I had a roommate in college who left for an 8:30 class, and I never heard from him again. He left without a trace. We came back one day and all his clothes were gone. He had just decided to move back home for some reason. Never did find out. Most unusual.

It's almost like marriage. You have to be equally yoked: not so much the spiritual aspect, even though it's important, but your temperament, personality, and the whole neat/messy thing. That could really get on your nerves and build up conflict over time when one person is so different from the other person. It's not that you're being insensitive or indifferent, you're just being who you are. In some areas, differences complement each other, and, in some areas, differences really clash. I'm more of a clasher.

Pets and That Added Responsibility
"Unconditional love wrapped in fur"

Lana—I think pets are great. I've had cats, dogs, a hamster, and even a pet rabbit. However, the pet rabbit didn't last too long. I was trying to potty train it to use a litter box. One morning my roommate got up to take a shower, stepped in rabbit poop, and that was that. I took it back.

Bethany (roommate #22) and I used to have two cats: WC and PC. WC stood for Whiny Cat. However, we didn't want to subject the cat to a self-fulfilling prophecy, so we hoped the WC would turn into Wonderful Cat. It didn't work. She was so lonely. So we got PC to be her "Partner in Crime." That really seemed to help. The difficulty arose when I decided to move out to live closer to my job. I took WC, and Bethany took PC. I didn't take to living by myself, and, since my new roommate was allergic to cats, I decided WC had to go. When Bethany heard that I was going to find WC a new home, it was like selling off my firstborn. She took WC back, and both cats are together again and living well in Chicago. Every once in a while, Bethany still tries to get me to pay cat support, but I haven't yet.

Soon after the cats were gone, I learned that I, too, am allergic to them. It finally clicked that it wasn't normal to have a continual cold. Now, I'd like to have a dog, but our landlord won't allow it. For now, I guess that's okay. I know it would be a lot of work.

Dana—Mufasa, the miniature Siamese with an attitude, and Molly, the well-padded, heavy-walking kitty, are very entertaining, but they are always trying to get where they are not supposed to be. I probably confuse my roommate's "children" because they have the run of the place, except for my room; so it makes it all the more tempting for them to run into my sleeping quarters through the partially cracked door when I am home and meow somewhat obnoxiously to announce their presence. Molly gently investigates the place, cautiously sniffing a book, a purse, the bicycle pedal, but not Mufasa. He suddenly becomes Spidercat—completely focused on the mission at hand—making calculated leaps from the floor to the dresser, over to the bookshelf, and landing at the final destination on the small, shaky table in the corner. Forget about maintaining that silk flower arrangement; Mufasa's new toy was soon to be captured, disassembled, tossed, and batted away, never to be seen again.

I don't mind pets. I just have always longed for a golden puppy with big, adorable doggy eyes who is full of energy (yet minds well) and is open to cooking me breakfast on occasion. It seems right now, though, as apartments and patios aren't as conducive to pet recreation as an open field of wildflowers, I wouldn't be able to offer the best for my furry companion. The confining apartment would be almost as bad as a cage—and that's not right. But for now, I have to admit, the cats keep me company.

555 Singles Surveyed

On the Topic of Owning Pets
Men   25% *do*
Women   42% *do*

Men have more dogs; women have more cats.

Nathan—It seems to me that a pet would be better than a roommate. No water after 8:00 P.M. so you don't wake me up too early for a bathroom run, you have to eat your dry Kibbles and keep your paws off my Starbucks ice cream, we watch only the TV shows that I want, and you stay in your cage while I'm at work. Seems like the perfect roommate to me. Yet, I have chosen not to do the pet thing. I am in a small apartment and just can't justify putting a yellow Lab through that. I am considering fish at the moment. They're tranquil, don't need to be walked, can live for a couple of days on one of those slow-release feeder pellets, and are more of a hobby than they are an adoption of a child. I suppose I like having control over my space. I parallel the pet purchase with the house-buying event. It just seems like a settled-in step to take at marriage.

Chris—Growing up, we had what I would call "disposable pets." They just seemed to die on us. I can't begin to count how many we went through. It is so foreign to me to hear that someone has had a cat for fifteen years. The longest time we ever owned a pet was three or four years, and too many were for fewer than six months. It seems morbid, I know, but we did care about each one.

We stopped naming them. We had several dogs called "Puppy." And we had several pets that had a different name from each of the eight of us. Maybe we confused them to death.

But Boogerhead was my favorite pet ever and the only one that was only mine. After I moved to Indianapolis, I was lonely and mentioned in class that I'd really like a kitten. The next day, a student, with her hands cupped, came in and set a very small kitten on my desk. It was the ugliest calico I had ever seen. It was so ugly it was cute, as Mom would say. I picked it up and looked into its face. It sneezed on me (thus, the name).

I would pet her. She would purr. We bonded. She was my only friend outside of school for a long time. She was a great kitten, and she grew into a beautiful cat.

After three years with Boogerhead, though, I had to give her to my sister in order to move in with my current roommates. Within six months, Boogerhead was nowhere to be found. We think she ran away. My sister must have gotten the "disposable pet" curse.

I yearn for a pet, though I don't miss the cat hair or the litter box. I know I'll have a pet later, when I marry. Most guys seem to like dogs, though. Dogs are okay, but I like my pets to sleep on my lap, while guys like to wrestle their pets for some reason.

Other Voices

Cherie Paliotta, Avalon—*I would love to have a pet again. I had a dog for sixteen years, but she just died this year. So I am in no shape for another emotional commitment to a pet.*

Max Hsu, Church of Rhythm—*Dogs are unconditional love wrapped in fur, but I don't have time for one right now.*

Rebecca St. James—*We have a goat, a dog, two birds, a rabbit, two cats, and some chickens. We've had at times up to thirty chickens, but I think the ranks are a little low right now because every now and then our dog will kill a couple of them. But we've got a lot of eggs. We give away a lot of eggs.*

Jaci Velasquez—*My dog is so spoiled that if he doesn't have my full, undivided attention, he gets sad and won't look at me. But I kind of cling to my puppy. If I were to find a guy just like my dog, I would be okay.*

Neat Freak or Slob?
"Once a week, I spend about an hour moving the piles."

Nathan—I like knowing that at this time in my life I have the freedom to choose what I can be compulsive about. I can decide if I'm going to be a neat freak or a slob. I seem to have been riding right in the center a lot in recent years. I am surface clean. When my small group from church first came to my apartment, the women marveled at how clean everything was. I asked, "What sort of state did you expect me to live in?"

"Most men are slobs. That's why I don't want to get married; I'll have to pick up dirty socks for the rest of my life," said one female.

"I can't stand the mess; I pick it up every week. And the bathroom, it's got to be clean," I replied. That's what I mean by surface clean. Everything appears neat and organized so that I can function and receive guests without too much cleanup time. But when I think about that filing cabinet in my closet, with a stack on top of it and a stack on the shelf above it and a stack on the floor, I get queasy. Because of this, I think I am a person with neatness on the brain. You know, when you sit at work and actually think about the state of your closets, there's something to be said about your personality. So I finally broke down and spent ten hours one Saturday making new files, sorting, reading almost everything, putting it all in its proper place. And now I feel relieved, sleep with a clean conscience, and am jubilant when I get my mail because I know there is a specific folder for each piece that doesn't get thrown away.

I wonder, if I were married, would I be able to dedicate that much time to a neat freak project, and, if so, would I be laughed at for smiling so much to myself out of contentment?

Chris—My bedroom—and my life, I guess—are cluttered. I think I have a latent fear of unpacking everything I own, really moving everything in, and putting it in its right place. Maybe some psychologist could explain that rationale. Someone, other than the good doctor, would probably just say that I'm lazy or have too much going on to finish my room completely.

I'm not a big neat freak. I had a roommate once who thought every Saturday was cleaning day. No, Saturdays are for sleeping in and having fun with friends. We never agreed on that point, and she'd often have the place spotless before I'd even poured my Cheerios.

My current roommates agree that the common areas should be kept fairly clean, while the bedrooms can and do look like a hurricane just went through the Great Plains.

Dana—Soon after Susan moved in, she came home to find my bills and other belongings spread out over the dining room table. Her panic-stricken eyes immediately caught my attention as she slowly scanned the room, wondering if this was a natural tendency of mine to keep my things out. . . . I quickly reassured her of the temporary chaos and of my desire to keep the shared living quarters in order. Our living, dining room, and kitchen are always clean and comforting. Comforting to me as areas to come home to and relax, knowing that everything is in its place.

Susan is so understanding when it comes to making sense of all my stuff. She continues to offer her assistance in an effort to develop an organizational system that works for my lifestyle. Meanwhile, my stuff can be silently concealed behind closed doors. I've often been accused of sleeping on "that closet you call a bed," complete with clean clothes mounds that almost seem like pillows. In my defense, at least they're clean. Sometimes I don't want to worry about it. Whether a good or bad thing, my time is just obviously spent elsewhere.

Lana—I am definitely not a neat freak, but I don't think I am a slob. I keep my things picked up in our common areas, but my bedroom is often a mess. My bed isn't made, and there frequently are piles around the room: a pile of clean clothes that haven't been put away, a pile of work clothes that were tried on but not worn, a pile of dirty clothes, and a pile of mail that has to be sorted. I know it would save time if I just would put things away, but I haven't been able to get that into practice.

Once a week, I spend about an hour moving the piles. I just can't make my bed each day. I'm the only one ever in my bedroom. The only time my bed is made is when company is coming and my bedroom might be on the tour. I know I feel better about myself when my room is clean, but when it comes to sleeping in a few more minutes or making my bed, the minutes win every time.

I'm an expert crisis cleaner. My family moved every four to five years. We knew the routine. The Realtor would call, and we heard the gun go off for the race to begin. I know how to hide things where the most curious of guests will never find them. The problem is that I often forget where I hid the items. The best addition to my bedroom was a rolltop desk that allows me to hide my paper pile.

We have a lot of people over to our house, and frequently they want a tour of our dwelling. We have a rule that we don't show someone's room unless the resident is present. There's good reason for that rule. One roommate has never forgiven me for giving a tour to one of our pastors. I showed him her room, and he was inadvertently exposed to her underwear on the floor. I doubt he ever saw it, but she has never been convinced.

Other Voices

Jeff Frankenstein, Newsboys—My parents were always telling me to clean my room, but as soon as I moved into my own place, I actually cared about it. It's weird. I painted it art deco green. I love old art deco furniture.

I didn't really have furniture the past few years. But now that we know we'll be there for a while, we're starting to fix it up. People are amazed that it is a bachelor pad, because it is so clean.

I actually cleaned my toilet for the first time in two years the other day. It was pretty exciting. Everyone gathered around. I took the scrub brush and went for it, and everyone cheered and stuff. It was pretty exciting.

Nikki Hassman—*I consider myself a clean person*—*not bragging*—*it's hard, because I am so busy. There is just not time to do a whole lot of cleaning. There is probably just one day in a two-week span where I have a little bit of time to clean, so naturally I am a clean person, organized. I have my closet color-coordinated.*

Mark Lowry, Out of Control—*There are some good things about being single. I don't have to clean out the refrigerator. I've got a piece of celery in there right now that's got longer hair than Crystal Gayle. I can scratch when I itch.*

I don't have to share my pizza. I can walk around in my underwear and not offend anyone but my Peeping-Tom neighbors. (And that just serves 'em right.) And I never have to change my sheets. Who cares? When one disintegrates, I put on another one. . . .

I've even learned how to save on laundry soap. I don't buy it. If I take my clothes and run 'em in the dryer long enough, they'll smell good again.[1]

Rebecca St. James—*I like to clean things because I like to see the difference you can make. Something is messy, but you clean it up and it looks nice. It's really fulfilling.*

Geof Barkley—*I try to keep my bedroom pretty neat and orderly. I don't know where I got that, but that is me. Love me for who I am.*

Janna Potter, Avalon—*My roommate knows. It's like a tornado hit her room. But she's great about keeping the door closed. It* doesn't go past her door. If I have to stay up till 2:00 in the morning to dust, I do—I am probably on the obsessive side. It really bothers me that someone could come in who has never been there before. That's one of my pet peeves, for somebody to come by and it be messy.

Michael Passons, Avalon—My roommate was an antithesis of me. I learned a lot of patience—how to let things go. I'd just count down the days until I could give that bathroom a big scrub. I had to hose it down.

Sometimes I wonder if I am too neat. You see these things on TV about these guys who straighten the fringe on their rugs. I'm not that bad, but sometimes I'll straighten it. I don't do it every day. If someone were to live with me, they would have to be like me, or we'd drive each other crazy.

Grover Levy—I've been labeled by someone as an anal retentive. I don't think my house necessarily reflects that. I like things to be pretty neat, though.

Gary Mullet—I figure if I can keep a path large enough to get from the doorway to the bed, I'm in good shape. It's not that bad, but it's probably the messiest room in the house. Nobody ever sees it but me. My room is entertainment central. It's highly focused for the single man. I've got the big entertainment center and my toys. I'm a total gismo freak—I got that from my dad. My bedroom is a miniature version of my living room: TV at the foot of the bed, stereo, and VCR. So I can lie in bed and be entertained for hours and never get up. The Nintendo is right there. . . . It's a little ridiculous actually.

Heather Floyd, Point of Grace—I'm messy. I've tried to be neat. I'm not gross messy. It's not like I leave food out, but I have piles of clothes on the floor that I haven't worn, instead of putting them back on the hanger, like Mom always insisted. I don't like the rest of the house messy. My roommate now is messy too. Just our rooms, though.

I can't stand to do laundry and have to put it up. I love clean clothes, but I hate folding them up and putting them away. They will sit in my laundry hamper folded neatly. Part of the reason is that I've accumulated so many clothes. My closet is bulging. I cannot say "no" to a bargain. Even if I don't need it, if it is on sale, I get it. So I have a closet full of great deals, and I wear probably a third of them.

Eating Habits
"Cereal for breakfast, cereal for lunch, and cereal for dinner"

Lana—My major food staple is Healthy Choice TV dinners. They go from the freezer to the microwave in the same box, and my only dirty dish when I'm done is a fork. I never read the calorie or vitamin information on the box. I want to trust the advertisers who say this dinner is healthy. My other two staples are cereal and nachos. For the nachos, I mix salsa with Velveeta Mexican cheese. Give me nachos with a cold Coke, and I'm in heaven. I don't dislike cooking, but it just isn't a priority for me when it is just me.

Chris—I stopped buying bread a long time ago. The family-size loaf would develop a lovely green fuzziness by the time I got halfway through it. Then I would wonder about the sandwich I ate yesterday. Did that green just appear overnight or should I not have been watching a recorded episode of *Friends* while I ate my sandwich?

One of my current roommates has nearly broken me of my

aversion to mold. It's kind of like violence on TV: the more you see it, the less repulsed you become.

I eat a lot of frozen and microwavable food. We order pizza, probably too much. And anytime I meet with someone, it is over a meal; so at least a few of my meals are out each week.

Dairy seems to be my downfall—cheese and ice cream, mostly. My mom said once, "Chris, milk is used to make little cows into big cows." She'd stop her comment there, but I could guess the rest. She couldn't come right out and call me a cow, you know.

555 Singles Surveyed

Have You Cooked a
Real Meal This Week?

45% Cooked 1 or Less

Dana—Just call me Queen of the Bread and Cereal Group. I love to eat and try to be health-conscious, but I never seem to eat consistent amounts of food at normal times during the day. As for specific eating tendencies, I usually start the day with a big bowl of boring, good-for-me cereal in skim milk. It's a good thing, because I do consume a large amount of bread (especially bagels, and the hot, buttery, French-loaf kind). Pasta dishes, rice, and vegetables thrown in here and there also seem to make up the majority of my food intake. I anticipate the weekends, though, for the time and opportunity to dine out and have some real food. And unlike some, I am not bashful; my dad raised us as a meat-and-potatoes family, and I wouldn't have it any other way. I'm never gonna be one of those gals who orders "a side salad and a small Diet Coke." I say, "Bring on the steak dinner with all the extras."

When dining at home à la Dana, convenience is the key. I wouldn't be able to function without that five-minute microwavable concoction. I'm usually starving when I get home from work at 6:00, and I'm too tired to break out the cookbooks and start producing beautiful platters. Okay, so the chance of ever creasing the cookbook binding is slim to none, but at least my rationale makes some sense. I just want to eat something—a little cheddar does wonders to those bland foods—and continue on with my evening of rehearsals and other happenings. Maybe at some point I will create culinary masterpieces, but for now peanut butter and jelly will have to suffice.

Nathan—Most of the guys I interviewed for this book liked to cook or at least felt confident they could whip up a little something if called upon.

Whenever our book group gets together for a writing session and we each bring our own eats, I bring food that I prepared. You wouldn't believe the marveling that goes on. I'm beginning to think women today are totally liberated from everything because a lot of the women I know don't even attempt to cook, and a lot of the men consider it a great hobby.

I make up big meals sometimes that I separate into lunches for myself, including everything from stir fry to pot roast, from hamburgers to pasta dishes. Just because I'm a bachelor doesn't mean I can't have a normal home life with cooked meals. One benefit to being a bachelor is that nearly every time I go home to eat with my parents, I return with a care package. I think health is too dependent upon diet to leave it all up to box meals. Those things are mostly carbohydrates. Where's the protein?

Other Voices

Max Hsu, Church of Rhythm—If it comes out of a can or we can microwave it, we eat it, grill it, nuke it, or something. I can cook. But we're just so busy. Cereal—we eat a lot of cereal. Cereal is good. You pour it in a bowl. You add milk. You're ready to go.

Heather Floyd, Point of Grace—I love to cook. I love to try new stuff. I don't get to do it too often, though. Last week I got out my cookbooks. I have recipes from Mom and my aunts. Good southern women cooking southern food—you know the stuff that's just bad for you.

All week I tried cooking some of these recipes. I wanted to be able to cook like they do someday. You know, without a recipe—all out of your head. I made pancakes one day and biscuits the next. They tasted right, but they did not look the same.

I called Mom and told her, "It tastes fine but my biscuits are droopy and flat." She asked if I used baking powder, and I said yes. Then I looked at the baking powder, and it had expired three years ago.

I eat pasta a lot. I don't want to buy groceries. I went on a diet and learned to cook healthy. I fixed dinner for my parents recently. After they said that it was good, I said, "Did you know that it is low fat and only three hundred calories?"

I try to eat breakfast. I don't always. I love pizza with ranch dressing. When I go to the movies, I have to get a Coke and a Nestlé Crunch in the little bunches. That's my movie meal.

I eat out a lot. The snacks I have at home are popcorn, Rice Krispies, and Milano cookies from Pepperidge Farm. Those are my favorite.

Jeff Frankenstein, Newsboys—I love veggie burgers. I like pasta. I try to cook as much as I can. We go out for Indian food a lot. One of my roommates is a baker, so he's always trying something, and I have a couple of friends who are chefs.

Rebecca St. James—I can eat reasonably healthy on the road. I'm not a dessert person, though I went through a phase not too long ago where I craved sweets like apple pie, and I thought, Oh no, this is not good.

I'll go through a time when I'm really into salads—like now. But sometimes I like potatoes. We do a lot of Wendy's. But I'm very much a breakfast person. I like to get up and get a bowl of cereal or porridge (oatmeal—we call it porridge in Australia). We drink a lot of tea. I could have up to three or four cups of tea a day.

555 Singles Surveyed

The Top 10 Favorite Cereals

1. Cheerios
2. Frosted Flakes
3. Life
4. Raisin Bran
5. Captain Crunch
6. Honey Bunches of Oats
7. Granola
8. Lucky Charms
9. Golden Grahams
10. Oatmeal

Mark Lowry, Out of Control—I love to eat. My favorite food is Mexican food. I was raised in Texas, and Texas has the best Mexican food in the world. . . .

Fat, greasy, crunchy, you fry it, I love it.[2]

Single and Content

Pam Thum—I don't like breakfast foods, but I love fish for breakfast! Not raw fish. I'm a big fan of homemade peanut butter and toast or an English muffin with butter—a lot of butter. I love vegetables. And chocolate. I do love chocolate.

Geof Barkley—It's hard because we're only in town for a day, and it is easier to run out to Subway. But if we know we'll be in town for a few days, we can go ahead and go shopping and have cereal. I have wasted more loaves of bread. There have been some serious science projects growing in my refrigerator.

Greg Long—I eat cereal. Yes, indeed. That's basically all there is in my cupboard. And it's all I do. I'll have Cheerios or Wheaties for the main course with bananas, and then I'll have Honeycomb for dessert. About as sweet as I can go would be Lucky Charms.

Michael Passons, Avalon—We're big fans of Steel Magnolias, the movie. We watch it over and over. There's this one part when Annelle wants to take something over to the Eastman house because Shelby just died. "I got to fix red beans and rice because it freezes beautifully. It's in the 'Freezes Beautifully' section of my cookbook." That's how I cook—so I can keep it a long time. I make great red beans and rice. You just throw it in the Crockpot and let it cook. I also get those Pillsbury cookies that you cut up then you sandwich with vanilla ice cream in between. Anytime someone comes over, that's what they want. It's like the specialty of the house.

Jody McBrayer, Avalon—We eat more than we practice. I like Italian food. I try to cook. I make great sweet tea.

Gary Mullet—I've been single long enough I actually cook pretty well—anything from one of those instant rice dinners to a roast, potatoes, the whole bit. I also love to grill, but I know it doesn't take much skill.

Grover Levy—When I cook for myself, it's not anything major; it's not anything more complicated than spaghetti or throwing a package of beans and rice on the stove and heating it up. Nothing better than beans and rice, man; I put a lot of stock in them.

Nee-C Walls, Anointed—You know what? I don't mind cooking, but I'm not into cooking, and I don't have to cook because I am single; I don't have anybody to cook for. I just don't enjoy it. But if I have to, I can slam up some breakfast food. And bread. I do love bread. I need to stay away from bread.

Jaci Velasquez—I like to cook, but I don't like to clean up; therefore I don't cook. When people ask me when they are at my house, "Where are the pans?" I'm like, "I don't know." I'm not much of the Suzie Homemaker. My mother is completely—all the women that I am surrounded by are Suzie Homemakers, and I am like, "Pfft. No thank you."

Mark Lowry, Out of Control—I was up north once and got into a discussion about food with a pitifully healthy-looking lady. "Oh, we don't overcook our vegetables up here," she said. "We don't want to cook the vitamins out of the vegetables."

"For goodness sakes," I told her, "take a pill and cook the vegetables!" You ever bite into a vitamin pill? They taste awful. You know why? Because they've got vitamins in them. That's why you need to cook those vitamins right out of those vegetables. They'll taste better. Forget the health nuts. We're all gonna be dead in a hundred years, for goodness sakes. COOK THE VEGETABLES![3]

The Fight against Flab
"Show me where Jesus ever jogged."

Nathan—Now is the time to be healthy. We are in the most control of our time and health when we are single. We have the power to say "no" to excess busyness and devote a portion of time to exercising and eating right. Why not be healthy? If you are trying to attract someone of the opposite sex, your odds of succeeding will be better if you are in peak condition. Face it, a big part of the whole dating scene is to attract someone. No matter how "Christian" your pool of dating resources may be, people's attention first has to be grabbed. You gotta look good. We all believe that true love means seeing a person's inner beauty, which is true, but how will they ever get to know that inner beauty if you can't make them notice you across a crowded room? I'm not here to give foolproof advice on improving your looks, but I believe we should maximize anything we've got.

I am always trying to resurrect my running circuit training routine, which has been dormant for nearly three months. I'm tall and lanky, but I could have some more muscle fairly easily if I just got committed.

I think that more singles go to fitness clubs since they are always looking for opportunities to mingle. Hence, they get more physical activity as a by-product of their naturally social inclination.

The flip side, though, is the whole eating habit arena. The single population must single-handedly keep the meal-in-a-box cartel humming along. I guess they're pretty healthy, but they seem to be full of a lot of sauce and are very expensive. When I first got out on my own, I bought one for each lunch of the week, but I found myself starving only an hour or two after eating one and could then be found raiding the vending machine for Snickers bars. I since have received nearly every small kitchen appliance invented and make most of my own meals, which I pack and carry with me. Now if they could just get rid of that frozen custard stand near my apartment, I would be a picture of health.

Dana—Waking up is my most immediate motivation for exercise. It's always helpful to remind the heart that it is still capable of beating at a higher rate than normal. Every morning is a constant battle to rise from under my soft, comfy, well-broken-in blankets. The thought of facing the often dark, early morning and the potential of scraping ice and snow off that igloo-once-known-as-my-car is not appealing. Once I'm up, though, I'm fine. I actually like exercising; it falls under that "in preparation for the new day" category, along with quiet time with the Lord. I feel so much better after riding my little stationary bike and repeating a few muscle strengthening and stretching exercises. The muscles in my legs are very tight (I have mild cerebral palsy and use crutches to walk) so any exercise contributes nicely to energy for the day—except I probably wouldn't be seen on those balance-required jaunts like rollerblading. It could be quite entertaining for spectators but not necessarily an enhancement to my workout routine.

Almost all of the singles I know are health-conscious and exercise frequently. I respect people, especially single people with often-inconsistent schedules, who set time aside to take care of themselves by exercising. Whether they physically need to burn those calories or not, it seems the positive benefits of trying to stay in shape make people feel better and therefore often more fun to be around. (I'd also like to think that I would be developing good long-term habits to avoid, as long as possible, that post-youthful flab.)

But don't get me wrong. I also think it's equally as important to have some lazy days. I'm all for hanging out on the couch every now and then watching a movie accompanied by my favorite junk foods. And I love to hit the dessert café for cheese-cake. But frequent stops for ice cream on hot summer days is the best. It certainly doesn't help control that sugar intake, but I think it's a great thing.

Chris—I want to be healthy. I do. But it is so hard. It's just so difficult to watch what I eat, exercise often, take vitamins, lower my stress, get enough rest, keep my skin moisturized, floss . . . and I wish that were all.

I don't think we can ever do enough for our bodies. We're never done. We can always be thinner, be more toned, eat bet-ter, think more positively, rest more efficiently, have smoother skin, or have cleaner teeth.

When the task seems so immense, it's easier to forgo doing those nightly sit-ups at my bedside.

555 Singles Surveyed

Do You Belong to a Health Club?

Yes 41%
No 59%

Lana—My biggest lesson regarding health issues came to me on a date. My date was explaining how his dad had died at a young age. He didn't take very good care of himself and died of a heart attack. I realized that not taking care of myself doesn't just affect me but all those who love me. One of the best gifts I could give to my future husband and children is to take care of myself. Biblically, my body is God's temple, so that should be motivation enough. However, sometimes I need people with skin on to help think about it.

I've been pretty lucky in that I don't have to work too hard to maintain my weight, but that doesn't necessarily mean I'm healthy. After that date, I developed a five-year plan. I figured that I couldn't change thirty years of bad habits overnight and have the changes stick. The first year, I started lifting weights. Year two, I added cardiovascular training, riding my bike or using my stationary bike. Year three was cutting back on caffeine. I used to have four or five Cokes a day. I'm now drinking one to two. I don't plan to get rid of caffeine completely. I think moderation is the key, and I love a good cold Coke! This year, year four, I'm trying to be more faithful in taking my vitamins and getting plenty of sleep. I also need to get back to doing the activities of the previous years more earnestly. It is so easy to backslide. Next year will be the all-time hardest: trying to eat better.

Other Voices

Heather Floyd, Point of Grace—*If I don't exercise I feel guilty. It's part of my daily ritual. I make it a priority. I enjoy it, and it makes me feel good.*

I cross-train—treadmill, walk/run, stairmaster, bike, weights. At first, I was hung up on the fact that if I lifted weights I would gain weight. But my trainer told me to get over it. One day I do arms then the next legs. I have a little routine down, and he's written it all out for me. I want to get into kick boxing or tae kwon do.

Mark Lowry, Out of Control—*Who invented exercise? Why do our bodies need it? Mine has done just fine without it for over* thirty years. I know our bodies are the temples of the Lord, but show me where Jesus ever jogged? . . .

I hate sports. There, I've said it. And it feels SO good. Besides the fact that I'm about as coordinated as a blob of Silly Putty, I have always hated any kind of activity that made me sweat.

I hate to sweat.

My idea of an exercise program is one sit-up a day. I do half in the morning when I get out of bed and the other half in the evening when I lie down.[4]

Jaci Velasquez—*I work out every day. I go on the treadmill for twenty-five minutes one day, upper body the next day, twenty-five minutes on the treadmill the next day, and lower body the following day. I don't work out when I am home, but when I'm on the road, I work out.*

Rich Mullins—*I just figure we're all gonna be dead someday anyway. You may as well go one way as the other. If you're overly obsessive about health, then you're dead already. What problem do you have that [death] wouldn't fix?*

Someone to Hang With
"Friends can become surrogate families."

Lana—When you're single, friends are the most important people in your life, next to a relationship, of course. Family is important, but those relationships aren't usually every day. My contact with my family consists of one phone call a week and getting together to celebrate this month's birthdays or significant holidays. I get together with my friends several times a week. We're eating out, catching movies, and just being social.

When singles get married, this friend/family time ratio does a 180-degree turn. Time with friends is curtailed, and much more emphasis is spent on quality time with the family. I think that's normal and appropriate. However, it sometimes leaves me feeling lonely until I find other friends to socialize with.

Singles are the most transient group of adults. In our singles' group at our church, 70 percent of those involved have only gotten involved in the last two years. This is true, even though our singles' group is thirteen years old. People are constantly getting married, taking a new job, or trying a new church. What this means for me is that I continually have to work at meeting people and developing friendships. If I don't, I can wake up and all my friends will have transitioned out of my life.

In TV and movies, it seems most friendships revolve around where people work. I have friends at work, but most of my friends are my college friends or those I meet at church. My best friends have been my roommates. Jodi is one of these. We've been roommates for over five years and have gone through job changes, death of family members, illness, and heartbreaks. We've shared our lives and still liked each other when it was over.

Dana—I love to laugh. One of the best things about my friends is that they encourage me and my many tangents; they allow me to be me. Of course, that's what friends are all about, caring for one another just because. I thank the Lord daily for blessing me with unique, loving friendships. I can't imagine life without them, and one of these friends is Leandra, whom I've known since second grade. From performing outdoor "concerts" for the parents, to acting out the tragic love triangle between her Ken and Barbie and my Farrah doll, to pelting the neighborhood boys in our victorious mud war games, we were virtually inseparable. Any normal situation eventually found us doubled over in laughter. And we looked out for each other. Knowing how much I, too, would have enjoyed a freshly packed lunch from Mom instead of enduring the scary school lunches, Leandra would always save her dessert snack for our long, rural bus ride home and split her treat with me (those chocolate cake, cream-filled SuziQ's were my favorite). Though many miles are now between us, we are always able to write or call each other and immediately pick up where we left off.

Since moving to Indianapolis, the Lord has brought exciting friends into my life, many of whom I have met through involvement in our church ministries. Whether hanging with my writing pals or the unique musicians from the praise and worship band, I have been able to share with them not only my interests, but, most amazingly, my faith in Christ. We study the Word, pray, fellowship, and worship together. We hold each other accountable, encourage one another, and care about each other's walk with the Lord.

I would drop just about anything for time with my friends to cultivate our relationships. Moments together are priceless. We've drunk homemade milkshakes while watching five consecutive *VeggieTales* episodes; we've sung praise tunes at night while on top of a houseboat among bats and shooting stars; and the gals and I have often retreated to warm our feet and sip hot tea in front of the fireplace, while profoundly discussing our take on men, relationships, and what we are learning from the Lord about His plan for our lives. The Lord commands us to love one another, and friendships like these seem to make that so easy. I am learning more and more how the Lord brings me so much joy through these friendships. I do feel blessed. And it's great to laugh.

Nathan—The week before Thanksgiving, I sat down around a table for a family-style banquet with eight people whom I didn't even know a year earlier. I was totally at home and excited about dinner with this "family." It wasn't a traditional family—

we were eight singles from our singles' ministry who had formed a small group for Bible study and spiritual encouragement. We had, in a very short time, become very close.

I only live an hour from my hometown but have tried right from the start to make Indianapolis my new home. By joining a singles' ministry focused on Bible study and building the most important relationship—the one with Christ—I quickly met others like myself and made lasting friendships. I'm convinced singles make friends easier than any other demographic group over the age of twenty-two. We are all in search of a place to belong, so we reach out more readily. Here we were at the banquet, people who didn't know each other a few short months earlier but had turned into a tight-knit group that met every week. We needed friends, so we made them.

A MAN OF MANY COMPANIONS MAY COME TO RUIN, BUT THERE IS A FRIEND WHO STICKS CLOSER THAN A BROTHER. —PROVERBS 18:24

I think in this stage of life, friends can become surrogate families. The humorous thing in our singles' ministry is the amount of eating out everyone does. We organize lunches after church, hang out in coffee shops after Sunday night classes, meet as small groups to study and have pizza, and meet up for breakfasts, lunches, and dinners outside of church activities. Eating alone isn't always fun, so we find friends and eat together.

This writing group was formed in just such a way. One of us on our newsletter team had a writing idea, and we started meeting every week to discuss the possibilities, share our writing, and, of course, help keep the pizza industry afloat. Then we started sharing personal struggles: my struggles with my job, Dana's decision to have major surgery, Chris's students, and

Lana's leadership positions in our singles' ministry. We prayed too. Then the work began. But it has been fun work because we have done it together—meeting to turn in assignments, getting together for five-hour writing and editing Saturdays, and yes, assessing each other's performance levels. We are learning to be accountable to one another. Doing all of this with friends has created more than a book for us, it has created a small community. Forever, when we get together, we will have this one thing in common to discuss and remember.

The small group from church has since disbanded and, for me, has been replaced with this writing group. But those friendships will last a long time. Although we see each other only a few times a year, we stay in touch.

Chris—You have to be a friend to have a friend, and I know I've let my friends down. Even a few broken promises block the building of trust. I need to be there. I should think of them more often than I do.

Lisa, one of my good friends, sends me cards all the time. She even sent me flowers at work when she knew I'd been going through a lot. Often she'll call in the middle of the week to ask how it's going.

> HE WHO ANSWERS BEFORE LISTENING—THAT IS HIS FOLLY AND HIS SHAME. —PROVERBS 18:13

As she struggled with her return to school full-time while still working full-time, I consciously had to tell myself to care. My busy life easily absorbs my thoughts.

Whether I'm with my friends or chatting with students, I am convicted by the question, "Are you listening, or are you waiting to speak?"

One of the perks of being a teacher is that I get to be friends with so many neat kids. All too often, I find myself taking on another project, when I could just "be" with them. I work at the computer while a student stands next to me telling me about boyfriend troubles or their home life. I could justify my actions by believing that I was listening, while my nonverbal feedback and soft words of encouragement are what they most needed.

I realize that I have to listen to my students, to my roommates, to all my friends. I need to be a friend to have a friend.

Other Voices

Max Hsu, Church of Rhythm—Something I've really learned lately is that friendship is everything. If you can be friends first, then God will grow what He will from the relationship, and, if that's a romance, then cool. Don't look for a mate. Look for friends.

Every day is a chance to love and to care and to say, "I'm sorry" or "I love you" or to take that step of vulnerability that we're afraid to take. Every day is a chance like that. We get so nearsighted sometimes.

When someone tells me something they've never told anyone else, that is a gift to us both. Man, when I die the only thing that is going to go with me is the lives I touched here on this planet.

Heather Floyd, Point of Grace—I have a friend whom I have just committed to pray for each time we brush our teeth. So twice a day I am praying for her and she for me to find the right person. My teeth are bloody because I'm saying, "Really, God."

Mark Lowry, Out of Control—Having friends who are a few bricks short of a load is great, too. I haven't had a normal friend in my life.[5]

Cherie Paliotta, Avalon—My friends mean a lot to me. I have a tendency to be like a mother hen to them. It's this instinct that God has put in me. I have some really good friends whom I would jump in front of a train for.

Dr. John Trent, Encouraging Words—It is really interesting that in Greek the word for life is literally the word "to move, movement." The reason is that something that is alive moves; it's connected; it has relationships. The word for death, thanatoss, is the word for isolation. Obviously, the ultimate isolation is death. Life is connection. Life is movement. Life is relationships. Death is isolation and separation. For singles in particular, the best way to develop relationship skills is to realize how crucial relationships are. It is a life and death issue. In Deuteronomy, the Lord says, "I lay before you life and death, the blessing and the curse." Someone may say, "I'm single, and that's a curse." It doesn't have to be. It's a choice: life or death, blessing or curse. The best thing you can do to prepare for a relationship is, number one, to realize that isolation is an enemy of life.

Mitch McVicker—The prayer I've been praying lately is that I open myself up to love, that I not be afraid of giving it to all people, and that I let love overcome my fears so that I can be an encourager to people. I think the biggest motivation people have is to protect themselves from suffering. But I've been praying that I can really open myself up to love, and then, come what may, because bad stuff will happen and good stuff will happen.

Jaci Velasquez—It's nice to be able to laugh with somebody and not feel like they are gonna think weird things about you, to be *able to do all the stupid things that you do. I think friends are probably the most special part of my life.*

Rich Mullins—*If I have to have perfect people in order to have friendships, I'm going to be a very lonely guy.*

The Need for Accountability
"Beyond the small talk"

Lana—I am really lucky to have had several spiritual mentors in my life: ladies who really cared, spent generous amounts of time with me, and held me accountable to God's design in my spiritual life. Cathy is one of those mentors. She discipled me when I was in high school. A young mom with two kids, she patiently worked with me. When I was in college, we continued to be close, even though my immaturity at times must have driven her crazy. When my first love broke my heart, she and her husband came the next weekend to encourage me. When she heard that I went to Purdue's Nude Olympics, she nailed me on it. I thought it would be fun to watch the "greatest spectacle in streaking," but she challenged me to think about my witness to my friends.

Our friendship has since transitioned. She's now more of a peer, but she still mentors me. We've been friends for more than fifteen years. When I owned my own company, Cathy was on my board. I know she loves and accepts me, but I also know that if she sees something wrong in my life she'll tell me. God encourages mentoring and accountability in His family. We are designed to need each other.

Nathan—At church, we have accountability groups. This organized form of accountability was somewhat new to me when I came to Indianapolis. In the past, I'd heard of people setting up accountability partners for help in specific areas: to make sure each was reading his Bible, that each one was staying away from a particular sin or trying to break a habit. But I hadn't been in a church that had a small group format. I think it sounds like a good thing.

Ultimately, we are all accountable to God. But in our humanness, we tend to need a person we can touch and feel who can look us in the eye to spur us to change our behavior. I have never set anyone up like that. I know in the small things, like getting up at 5:00 A.M. to run or show up at a gym consistently, I have always been more successful when I knew someone else was waiting for me.

As singles, without a spouse to act as that natural accountability partner, I see a lot of people get involved in accountability groups. They're usually separated into groups for women and groups for men. It sounds like a tough thing, to talk about your weaknesses with other people. But what a family we have in Christ, to be able to do this and not suffer scorn, but be taken by a loving hand and helped through a particular situation.

Ultimately, we are accountable not only to God but also to each other whether or not we set others up as our accountability partners to witness our thoughts and actions. By being a part of this family, we are accountable to a certain set of actions and thoughts based upon our belief in the Lord Jesus Christ as part of the Trinity and our risen Savior.

Chris—A friend in college said that he would hold me accountable in an area where I was struggling. That year I learned that accountability isn't always easy or fun. It is giving someone else the permission to discipline you, to point you on the straight and narrow. And that is what my friend so graciously did.

He would end our time together by asking, "What are you afraid to tell me or worried that I'll ask you about?" In a caring environment, this question could bring out so much beyond the simple answer, "I'm doing okay."

I dreaded one question over all the others, though.

"So, how are you doing [in a certain area] on a scale from 1 to 10?" he'd ask after some small talk.

I guess it comes from the teacher mentality, but I graded myself on a scale. But at the same time, I would allow for improvement. So, the answer was always, "Oh, I don't know. Maybe a 7 or an 8."

Maybe it came from trying to be accountable to a guy. Maybe he was too analytical, where I needed more compassion and tenderness.

But we all need someone to keep us in line, to tell us when we have broccoli in our teeth or we are dating the wrong guy, to encourage us to go beyond what we think is possible. A friend is someone who really knows us, yet sticks around and even likes us.

Like Martin Luther King Jr. said, "In the end, we will remember not the words of our enemies, but the silence of our friends."

Dana—I try to be accountable first to God, to seek Him first in any situation. This is a difficult challenge for me, though, because I often immediately want to open up to a close friend, to that tangible person who can quickly verbalize a response, and then seek reassurance from the Lord. When I struggle with having effective study time in the Word or being motivated by my own agenda instead of opening my eyes to God's perspective, I need to take these things to the Lord in prayer. I believe it is so important to be accountable to someone for my thoughts and actions, and, right now, that number one person is the Lord.

Beyond those wonderful, yet convicting, discussions with my mom, I guess I have never really had a Christian woman mentor in my life to whom I was specifically accountable. I've just kept to myself, assuming that my roommate or another close girlfriend would bring to my attention where I'm deviating from the Lord's will.

Many people in our singles' ministry talk about their involvement in accountability groups. I believe the overall intention is positive, but I sometimes wonder how healthy it is to share sensitive issues in a group setting. And does confidentiality become a consideration? Maybe it isn't best to voice personal concerns about family or friends to more than one set of ears at one time; general prayer requests might be more helpful. I realize we all need to be accountable to someone, I just hope that people seek appropriate, godly counsel.

Other Voices

Rich Mullins—It is vital for everybody not to live independently from authority. That's when someone who is a little older or a little further down the road can help us. All good authority should point us to God. When you're a young Christian, there are a lot of decisions that are really good for someone else to make for you, until you mature to a point where you're able to sense the leading of the Spirit. One thing they can do is help you learn to obey, which is I think the biggest struggle in the Christian life.

Heather Floyd, Point of Grace—Pray that God will send you someone to keep you accountable. He will do that if you want it. He'll put people across your path. Some are obvious, like friends. They need to ask good questions, hard ones. "What are you struggling with right now?" It's hard to have someone in your life do that.

These would be the friends who are the deeper ones, beyond the small talk. These are the friends for life, whom you allow to see your heart and soul.

Rebecca St. James—My family is a pretty major source of accountability because they know me so well, only second to God really, and will feel free to challenge me when I'm getting selfish or when some of my perspectives or attitudes might not be what they think they should be. I appreciate that so much. Sometimes at first, it's kind of frustrating. But I look back and realize they were right.

Jeff Frankenstein, Newsboys—We're pretty quick to bring each other in line. It doesn't really happen that much. We all spend as much time as we can in the Word, reading, usually not together. Our bus driver is a pastor, so he's there if we need him.

Jaci Velasquez—I'm more of a family accountability person. If my parents see something that is not good in my life, they will call me on it. That is a good thing.

Larry Burkett, Christian Financial Concepts—People generally marry their opposite; for instance, one is a late-night person, the other an early-morning person. One is a spender, the other a saver, and so on. This provides a good balance that most singles lack. There's no one to hold them accountable. Therefore, it's very important for single adults to find someone to provide financial feedback to balance their decisions. And it should be someone who is their exact opposite. This will help equip them later for marriage.

2

God Gave All of Us Twenty-Four Hours in the Day

(Work and Ministry)

It comes out of nowhere. That annoying monotone buzzing of my alarm pierces my ears, cuts straight through my pleasant dream, and disrupts all serenity. I have to get up. I have to work. I want to feel positive about my glorified customer service job, but somehow, I just can't get motivated to sit in my tiny cubicle, answer call after call, and interact with stressed-out coworkers.

Other singles my age seem to have successful, fulfilling careers, with plenty of savings in the bank and time to vacation and take it easy every now and then. Meanwhile, I'm constantly playing catch-up: the bulk of my paycheck goes straight to bills, I feel no creative freedom in my position, the benefits leave much to be desired, and I never quite feel relaxed when I do get a break from the office. Where is my free time?

Yep, I'm whining. But what started as a temporary job after college has lasted over three years so far. I keep waiting on the big neon sign from the Lord that would tell me my next step. I'm struggling to stay positive. However, God is starting to teach me that His timing is not my timing. Even though my job isn't great, I have so much to be thankful for. I can pay my bills. I do have Fritos on the counter and ice cream in the fridge. I have friends and family who love me. I have a purpose beyond my nine to five.

I might not have creative freedom in my job, but God has allowed me to be creative in the way I serve Him in church. I help plan and lead worship on Sunday mornings. Three others and I sing in a group called SALT, Sharing A Living Testimony, where we try to minister to each other as well as to those who hear us sing. I'm active in my singles' group. The Lord wants us to serve Him first, not ourselves. I'm trying to view the Lord as my employer and be proactive in my spare time. I actually look forward to the mornings. But I could do without that annoying alarm.

Affording Good Money Decisions
"I'll pay it off at the end of the month."

Nathan—I have always wished that I could fulfill that stereotype of a single male: great career, super car, some money to burn, snappy dresser. But I make my living as an artist, which, in reality, means: okay job, trustworthy car, can go to dinner a couple of times a month if I plan ahead, generally have something clean to wear. I knew it would be somewhat like this if I chose art for a profession. Designers, unless they work for a hot firm on Madison Avenue, don't make too much money.

So, I'm always looking for that one big idea that will either launch an uncommon career or be a big shot in the arm as a sideline. I helped start an outdoor lighting display company, only to find out the sales manager couldn't be trusted. Two years after I pulled out of the corporation, I am still waiting for my cut for the startup designs I created. I went off to a five-day, intensive real estate school to learn how to buy cheap and sell at market value but found out it would be nearly a full-time job for at least three years to get it going. I seem to always be pulled into someone else's scheme for a startup business, donating my time to receive a cut in the end: like a guy from my church wanting to market prepaid phone cards. I designed three credit cards for him that I am almost sure he used, but I never saw any money.

The one thing that I pray to learn is the ability to save. I used to be a great saver in high school and college. In college, I paid for three trips abroad. Even though finances weren't tough for me, I could have easily spent the money I earned at the pizza place but instead was able to sock it away. Even now, I'm not a big spender. But the act of living—rent, utilities, car, groceries—seems to sap my measly salary. I see a lot of my friends buying houses, going to Italy over Christmas break, getting a second car, and I wonder how they are doing it. Then I remember, they are married. They have two incomes, and generally one of those incomes starts soaring right about now because that individual (usually the man) has the luxury of nurturing it with nearly all his time. Then I have to rein in my own wants, realizing that until I can come up with that one big idea, for now I am a one-income household and have to stop trying to live like I'm not.

But that all sounds too depressing. Really it's not. God and I are in charge of all the funds in this household. I pray that God helps me be a steward of what He has entrusted me, that I budget well and spend thriftily. But if I make any mistakes, I truly have to go only to Him for forgiveness and to no one else. That's the freedom that singleness provides me right now. No one has to look at that checkbook balance but me and God. I know that I can live independently, not having gotten married right out of college and diving into a two-income lifestyle. I've learned how to stretch a buck, how to use tuna fish and peanut butter creatively, and how to entertain myself on a three-day weekend around town. I have to look at the residual blessings in the situation. I have learned a lot. I'm sure that if I had married right out of college and bought a house I would have learned a whole other set of lessons, but, in His infinite wisdom, God knew that these were the lessons I needed to know.

Lana—I'm glad that many of the money lessons I've learned have been while I'm single. I would hate to have my financial blunders affect a spouse or my children. My biggest blunders have been not counting the true cost of a decision. I moved out of my parents' home after college without realizing how much life would cost. Moving back with Mom and Dad was one of the most humbling times of my life. They were very gracious, but I felt like a failure.

Probably the next biggest lesson was controlling my impulse spending. I am very prone to the power of suggestion. Just yesterday I bought a Twix candy bar because the night before, it was the featured item in a *Seinfeld* episode! I've learned that I need to stay away from magazines and catalogs or just shopping to shop. I'll see something that I never thought I'd want, and I'll really want it. I'll either buy it when I shouldn't and feel guilty, or I won't buy it and will be frustrated because I really wanted it.

Just recently I've taken a good step toward better financial management. I attended a Crown Financial Study, which helped me to understand God's view of my stewardship. I am responsible to Him for how I spend 100 percent of the money given to me, not just 10 percent.

The last five years, I've done really well at keeping track of where my money goes, using financial software. But controlling it before it goes is a different thing. I've completed my budget and am trying to keep it in check. The big items that I have the hardest time controlling? My entertainment and dining budget is the most out of balance. I've started trying to bring my lunch to work, but, boy, I'd rather have someone else do the cooking. My computer is another challenging area. Because I am a computer consultant, it's easy for me to rationalize software purchases because it makes me more marketable.

Dana—Sometimes I think it's a shame that money has such an impact on the way we live and feel about life. I am thankful that I am able to pay the bills, feed myself (although my taste buds have given in to my cooking and are no longer particular about meals), and maintain necessary clothing for the change of seasons. I can definitely say I have never had an abundance of money, but as my practical years of singlehood continue to show, I have not been in need. Sure, I have been in want. I would like to make enough money to be more comfortable and not to live on such a tight budget, but I have gotten used to my financial situation for now and am learning to stretch my dollars.

I have seen how unhealthy financial situations can cause personal tension, hinder family relations, or strain a marriage, and I never want money to dictate or run my life. I believe it's all about budgeting and living within my means. Sure, there are many things I would like to be doing with my life that money could facilitate, but I have to look at where God has me and accept where I am. It is so tempting to compare myself to others my age, knowing that they have successful careers in their fields, but I now refuse to measure my worth according to the paycheck I receive. The Lord is teaching me what it really means to work for Him and find my identity in Christ. He wants me to quit complaining about unimportant material things and reach out to others. I am enjoying life, developing relationships, and making it on my own. So things aren't exactly the way I thought they would be financially. The Lord keeps telling me to depend on Him completely. My life, whatever the monetary situation, is proving a testimony to His provision and goodness.

My prayer is for others to develop a healthy attitude about money and to budget and seek the tools necessary to keep it under control. Eventually, I would hope that the focus could be on giving back to the Lord and not on struggling to make ends meet. We have too much work to do for the Lord to be painfully controlled by dollars.

Chris—My graphic arts teacher once showed me his paycheck. "You don't want to go into teaching," he pleaded. "You're too smart for that. You can do so much more."

He warned me that teaching would never fill my pockets or give me everything I would want out of life. So far, though, teaching has given me everything I could want. I'm not starving. I can pay my bills. I'm making a difference in the lives of a hundred and fifty teenagers a year. I have a ministry there. I've never regretted going into teaching, and I know it is where God has placed me for now.

This doesn't stop me from comparing myself to others, though. My sister, with a GED and six months' training, has a job in a hospital and is making more than I do. So many of my friends are able to buy nice sports cars, while, until recently, I could only afford junk cars. (I called my last one my "leprosy car" because the paint on the hood flaked and peeled.) I have a few friends who are my age or younger with new homes tastefully decorated, while I'm still renting and still decorate my room with posters.

The number of references to money in the Bible comes second only to the word *love*, and Jesus spoke more on this topic than any other. It seems that He wants us to understand its danger.

I've seen contentment on my trips to Mexico. The people we build the houses for have nothing. The children wear the same clothes each day, yet they run around giggling with their friends. The small gifts we give to the families bring tears as the mothers accept them. We cry with her not only out of pity, but also from guilt. We could have given more of ourselves. We could have brought them more than a few bowls and dish towels. As we hurried to pack the many unneeded items for the trip, could we have thought a little more about whom the trip was for?

In America, we feel that everybody owes us something. In Mexico, they don't expect anything. They live for the day.

We deserve nothing. We can survive with much less. We can be humbled by thinking on these things.

Other Voices

Grover Levy—*I think money affords you the flexibility to make some decisions that somebody else with a family might not be able to make; in other words, I can be out on the road because there's nobody here at home who depends on me for their well-being. And financially, I'm only responsible for myself. I can make some financial decisions without the pressures of having to provide for a wife or children.*

Cherie Paliotta, Avalon—*I charge. It's not good. I know one thing for sure about my husband, whoever he is: he's got to be very good in business. He's got to be. If not, we're going to be in big trouble. Math is not my thing.*

Max Hsu, Church of Rhythm—*As missionaries, my parents don't make any money either. So it's kind of funny. But they tell me, "You should be stable" and all this stuff. And they're in Hong Kong. It's a very unstable climate, with the change back to communism.*

I told them frankly, "I do as you do, not as you say." I made them a deal. If they'd come back from Hong Kong, I'd quit music. We're kind of at an impasse.

Heather Floyd, Point of Grace—We try to be wise with money. *Wise people counsel us. If we decide not to sing ten years from now, then we won't have to worry about it.*

Don't tarry; do it now. Dad was always good with teaching me about money. When I wanted to buy a car, he said to take this amount monthly from my account and see if I could live without it, then I saw that I could afford it and I had a down payment. It's very wise to invest. There are so many options nowadays. Dad always says that he wishes he had invested earlier. If he had at twenty-five, he'd be so much better now for it. I don't know much about it, but I do know that it's best if you start young.

Larry Burkett, Christian Financial Concepts—*[We forget] that God owns everything, and we are simply His managers or stewards. Psalm 24:1 says, "The earth is the LORD'S, and the fulness thereof; the world, and they that dwell therein" (KJV). As good stewards, it's important for us to manage the resources God gives responsibly. We can't do that if we're spending more than we make.*

I recommend that single people save at least 5 percent of their income, and this is not escrow money intended for later bills. It has been my observation, though, that most single (never-married) adults seem to have the least difficulty with saving money. They usually do quite well.

Insuring Yourself
"Be prepared so that you're not a burden."

Chris—Mom and Dad didn't maintain my insurance when I went to college, and I didn't see the need to pay for my own, since the few visits to the college health center were a cheaper alternative. However, in my junior year, I started having headaches and even fainting spells. It was difficult to concentrate, and my head tingled. I went through more than a year of costly tests, tests that the health center couldn't do. The doctors tested me for epilepsy and, although that test was not conclusive, put me on medication. The pills made me worse, though. Then they tested me for Lyme disease because I had spent the previous summer in Michigan. Before I gave up, I had undergone three tests for Lyme disease, a couple of blood tests, two EEGs, and an MRI.

We still aren't sure what infected my body that year, but I slowly improved by eating better and decreasing stress. However, as bills started rolling in, the stress level was difficult to keep down. I never knew that when you go to the hospital you get bills from each department separately. As a junior in college, I had already put myself in considerable debt. I only went to the doctor a few times and only out of desperation. Maybe I could have gotten better sooner if I had gone sooner for help.

It did teach me a lesson, though. I'll never go without medical insurance again.

Lana—I think most people purchase insurance to protect their loved ones rather than just themselves. Because never-marrieds typically don't have dependents to consider, many singles don't really think about buying extra insurance. We insure our things—cars and apartments or houses—but we rarely think about ourselves—purchasing disability insurance or having additional life insurance. I purchased disability insurance a couple of years ago. I realized that disability insurance was probably more important than life insurance at this stage of my life. My life insurance will be enough to bury me and pay off my debts. However, if I am disabled, I am not sure who would take care of me.

Single adults also need to have a will and have their estate in order. I don't have everything in place, but I have begun to get my records in order and have started to work on my will. By having these things in order when I die, I will alleviate some struggles for my family.

I think of the tragic car accident of Rich Mullins and Mitch McVicker. It was Rich's time to go. Mitch has undergone extensive medical attention and therapy. When I place myself in either of their situations, I have to ask, Am I ready?

Nathan—I did a little research to substantiate a claim we had about singles and car insurance. I was suspicious about the idea that singleness increases a customer's premium. What? We're all such wild and crazy guys and gals that we just can't settle down and get married, so that is an indicator that we are risky liabilities in an automobile? The craziest thing I have done in the last six years is drive while eating an Arby's Roast Beef and Cheddar and dipping fries in ketchup placed in the passenger seat, and I've seen married people do that too!

When I was about twenty-five, I called around to try to get lower auto insurance rates. One agent started out by saying, "You already have two strikes against you by being a male at age twenty-five. Please tell me you are married." By being unmarried, I guess, my rate went up even more, so I stayed with the insurance company I currently was with.

Dana—I never imagined that I would ever be so concerned about the details of insurance coverage, but the summer of 1997 changed everything. The consideration of three major surgeries over the course of two years caused me to sit up and take notice. I have had mild cerebral palsy since birth, which affects my motor movement and muscle tightness in my legs. Though cerebral palsy is not degenerative, I always assumed that beyond the minor, but positive, effects of strengthening and stretching exercises, I was pretty much stuck with my distinct pair of limbs and unique approach to walking.

I had three corrective surgeries in the first thirteen years of my life, but I never had to worry about operation expenses and insurance. It was a family effort, and my parents worked everything out. But as a twenty-seven-year-old single female under my own insurance, things had to be handled differently; I was now assuming the responsibilities of my long-awaited independence. In consideration of upcoming surgeries, I scheduled my doctor appointments, collected and reviewed the literature, and asked all the questions. Realizing the benefits of and potential for surgery, I began contacting the insurance company, talking with agents, and seeking approval for possible procedures. Suddenly I found myself in the middle of overwhelming details, scheduling issues, and weeks of waiting. I became extremely familiar with my insurance policy and the type and length of coverage and had to consider the possibility of making premium COBRA payments. After much legwork, praying, and scheduling, I was finally confirmed for surgery.

Because the doctor told me I would be unable to work for three to six months, I resigned from my job and prepared for those extra monthly premium payments. Unfortunately, disability insurance would not go into effect until a year after that surgery, so efforts for that type of coverage were put in place in preparation for a third and final procedure, if necessary.

The details were amazing. I learned quickly how to ask the right questions and go out of my comfort zone to get what I needed from the insurance agents. Sure, it might have been easier for my parents or my spouse (if I had been married) to handle everything and take me out of the equation, but the Lord gave me the strength, the comfort, and the endurance I needed daily to get things accomplished. He was, and continues to be, so faithful as I am currently in the middle of the challenging surgery process. He has brought me to a place of trust and faith in Him that I have always longed for. But I found I had to relinquish control of everything and let Him lead. I never thought my dealing with insurance would teach me so much about myself and even more about His sovereignty. The focus turned away from the surgery and right to the Lord, where it should be.

Other Voices

Larry Burkett, Christian Financial Concepts—Disability insurance is very important, especially for young single adults. If a single is out of work for more than the allotted sick days, he or she has no one else to pay the bills. However, savings of at least three months' wages will eliminate the need for disability insurance in most cases.

Working Hard for the Money
"I tend to think success is overrated."

Lana—It has never really been my goal to be a career woman, but the older I get and since marriage is not yet seen on the horizon, I don't feel I have a choice. How can I be a housewife when it is just me? Honestly, I am not sure I'd want to be a housewife, but I would like the choice.

Actually, I guess I do have choices. I can choose to focus so much on my job that it becomes my life. I can choose how much of my identity comes from my job or from who I am in God's eyes. I can choose to strive for excellence in all that I do and never compromise integrity. God gives me many choices. I probably shouldn't complain that I don't have the choice of not working. Most people don't have that choice either. I just need to make the most out of the choices He provides.

I've never been affected by this personally, but I have heard that marriage implies stability and maturity. Some companies consider this as part of their evaluation. Often, I've heard it said that, in scheduling, some companies would give the harder, less convenient work shift to the single adults, because they don't have the family commitment.

I don't think my singleness affects my job or that I am treated differently. In fact being single helps make some parts easier to bear. Where I work, we sometimes have to work six days a week. It is easier for me to adjust to a shorter weekend than the married women I work with. They have much more to juggle. However, they get to go home to their husbands, and I am too tired to go out and meet Mr. Right.

Dana—I always thought I would have a handle on my career soon after college. Well, think again. I guess the Lord had other things in mind. I have voice and journalism degrees from Indiana University, and upon graduation, I had to return to my nice, but small, hometown (complete with wheat fields and cow pastures) in southern Indiana. In fact, both my brother and I were back under our parents' roof. What an awkward situation. I had to find a job. In August, I worked part-time at our church as the choir and youth director. While maintaining this job, I moved to Indianapolis for a marketing communications internship. I thought this internship would create leads and launch my journalism career, but I found myself seeking a pay-the-rent job so I could stay in Indianapolis. I did find a job, but it contained minimal responsibilities that would utilize my journalism skills. As for music, my church has provided an outlet for my singing through serving as a praise and worship leader and with a vocal group born out of our singles' ministry.

The Lord has taught me a lot about patience and character-building experiences while enduring my less than ideal, but experience-building, full-time job. All along, I have been praying for time to focus on music and writing. After almost four years, I am finally able to concentrate specifically on these things, but I didn't know this much-wanted time would take the shape of surgery and three to six months away from work in a wheelchair. I left my full-time job to concentrate on corrective surgery and recovery. Meanwhile, God has given me this time to focus on writing and music. The Lord amazes me. Even though I still have no specific career after college, He is directing me and giving me the tools to do His work. I still sing consistently on our singles' and contemporary service worship teams and am excited about pursuing music ministry. And there's much work to be done on our book project. I never would have imagined being able to write about my singleness. The Lord knows what He is doing. I have no idea what my official career will end up being. I've heard it changes many times during our lives anyway. Right now, I'm plugging away: moving forward but not really trying to make sense of it all.

555 Singles Surveyed

Do You Have a Bigger Workload
Because You Are Single?

Most of the Time   16%
Some of the Time   40%
Never   44%

Nathan—When I first started my job, I felt I had to be there until the bitter end to see a project successfully out the door. I was in charge of producing all the book cover designs that were developed in our department. Designers would come up with concepts, present them to editorial and marketing, essentially sell the ideas, and then hand them off to me to put together, copy-fit, manage through a lengthy approval process, prepare the final electronic file for the vendor service who would output our negatives, and troubleshoot any problems that might arise at that point. I was perfect for the job: single, totally unattached, and wanting to establish a place for myself at this company. If I didn't handle it, nobody else would, as I was the only person with this job description and ability. Plus, I couldn't stand the thought of something I had touched not going perfectly. It was common for me to work a fifteen-hour day and very common to put in a twelve-hour one; a ten-hour day was standard. I came in an hour early, which was generally two hours before the designers, ate my lunch while pecking at my computer, and stayed at least an hour past 5:00.

Then somebody else with my job description was hired, and my workload decreased some, but not a lot, because the volume of work was increasing rapidly. Finally, three of us were doing the same job, and all of us were very busy. I don't think any of the designers or managers truly expected more of me simply because I didn't have a family, but I thought that I should take up the slack so the design staff, who had families, could get home. I believe wholeheartedly in people putting family first, and I was enabling them to do that, I felt.

The point is, I was willing and my late hours were okay because I was imposing them on myself. The other two or three people handling production put in long hours, too, so I didn't feel it was necessarily unfair; it was just a job that took longer than others.

I think that I established myself as a person willing to go the extra mile when needed, but I eventually ended the ludicrous hours I was working and hinted that we needed more clones of me. And we got them. I hope that this attribute, the willingness to stay late, had some impact on my coworkers. I want them to feel that they can rely on me.

I've learned that in many companies singles, not their married counterparts, are being expected to fill that extra time need. Sounds like we are going to have another trod-upon person-group uprising. Fair's fair. I can agree that a job should be no respecter of marital status, and if there is an extra flux of work, everyone—married or not—should divide it equally. I pray that if I find myself in this sort of situation, I can put in the time for my married coworkers to give them freedom to go home at 5:00 but that I will also be able to point out diplomatically that we all need to put in a little extra time at the computer.

I think that singles might throw themselves into work a little more than marrieds do. It's the one thing that, for non-Christians, defines them to the world. I can see singles committing to a career instead of a spouse, nurturing a career instead of children. I personally think that, given the situation, we do have the luxury of developing a well-polished career, but, like everyone, we should be reminded of the need for balance.

Chris—I'm not asked to work harder because I'm single, but, because I have no one to rush home to or any schedules to work around, I can stay late at school. These are some of my best times.

I know it happens, but I don't understand how someone can have my position as newspaper and yearbook adviser and be married with a family. Sometimes I think that is why God hasn't brought someone my way yet. Or is it that I'm at school too much to meet many available, Christian men?

Being the only single teacher in a high school makes life interesting. It's amazing to me that kids are no less concerned about my marital status than my family.

When a man walks in my room for something, as soon as he leaves, the kids giggle and ask me if that was my boyfriend. Really, it gets annoying. One time it was a dirty guy in coveralls wanting my signature before picking up our recyclables. Another time it was a construction worker checking on his work. A guy walks in, talks to me for a second, and leaves, and the whole room buzzes with questions about him.

Other Voices

Cherie Paliotta, Avalon—*I have pretty much made a mental decision that I don't want to get involved with anyone who cannot handle or support my ministry, because this is where God wants me to be for this season of my life.*

Jeff Frankenstein, Newsboys—*The advantages are unbelievable. I've seen more of the world than most people see in their entire lifetimes. Meeting so many people every day you really learn a lot and grow a lot. Sometimes it's weird after coming off the road for a long time. It's kind of hard to relate to normal life, and I miss that sometimes. But I'd say the advantages are well worth it.*

Max Hsu, Church of Rhythm—*I'm in one of those interesting jobs where what I do is kind of fun. So I don't know when I'm not working or when I'm working.*

Geof Barkley—*Being single has allowed us to buy more gear. Your wife would kill you. I bought just beaucoup stuff this year. I see the married guys, and the Lord has blessed them. But it is so hard for them to go on the road and leave those young ones behind and their wives to take care of things. I know God promises that there is a special blessing for those who leave home to serve Him, but I know how hard it is for those guys.*

The downside of that is that loneliness still permeates when you're on the road or when you're at home.

Pam Thum—*I was kind of shocked when my managers told me, "Well, here's another one that I think is trying to book you to date you."*

I was like, "Oh, so they don't really want me." I've gotten some letters from people who felt like it was God's will for us to get together. They saw me on a TV show and recognized qualities they wanted in a wife. Then they think, That's the girl for me.

Janna Potter, Avalon—*It's exciting, but I think there are days when you wake up and you don't really know where you are. Or you are so tired that you don't know what day it is. You talk to some artists and they make it sound like it's so hard, but I just don't think that it is, most of the time. I think we are very privileged and grateful that God allows us to do this because it is what we love to do and what we feel called to do, most importantly, but it's also our passion in life.*

Rich Mullins—*I tend to think success is overrated, that it's something everybody goes after until they get it, then nobody knows what to do with it.*

Michael Passons, Avalon—*It's great that we all are single now because of how much time is demanded to do what we do. We are on the road a whole lot, and when we're home we're still not home. We're working in studios and this and that. I think that would really strain a marriage. If Avalon were two or three years down the road—when we didn't have to travel as much—it would be different. But now it's new, and we are trying to get the word out. We really are pushed to the limit time-wise.*

Time Management
"I wasted an hour watching Rosie."

Chris—I'm currently going through a devotional guide called *God's Abundance: 365 Days to a Simpler Life.* Each day it offers insight from well-known Christians on how they've simplified their life, then it gives one tip to put into practice.

But too often I miss a couple of days then rush through three days' worth of suggestions to simplify my life. I think I miss the point.

I've always had trouble saying "no" when asked to help with something, join something, or do something. I am getting better, though. For a couple of years, every night was filled on my calendar. I now have a few nights off, though I feel a bit lazy dealing with unstructured time.

God has taught and retaught me that He wants me more than He wants what I can do for Him. I've always worked on a great résumé instead of my relationship with Him. I'm trying to learn to *be* instead of *doing* it all.

But I think being busy, whether it is in ministry or work, is easier for the single because we have more time. Busyness is also our solace when we're lonely. And when I run to that solace, I become lonelier, because I haven't shared who I am, only what I can do.

Lana—Most personality tests or profiles have one dimension that compares individual tendencies to focus more on tasks or relationships. I am a task person. I'm trying to be more of a people person because people matter to God. However, I think tasks matter to God too. The challenge is to get the right tasks accomplished and nourish the right relationships. In the time management planner area, there are many different types: Franklin, Daytimers, etc. I use Stephen Covey's personal planner

Hard to Do Single

We would love to live in a world where we didn't have to think about car problems, trash, handling bugs or dead animals, or loosening stubborn lids. Guys seem to feel like guys when we hand them a jar and say in a pouty voice, "Open this." Or when they rescue us from the spider in the kitchen. Or when we can't lift some heavy object or figure out why our brakes are squeaking. We say let them feel smart, strong, and needed. Let them feel like guys.

Other Snags of Singledom

- There's no one to yell at you when you hit the snooze for the fifth time.

- When water is gushing and a minor flood is forming, who can I call besides Dad?

- It's hard to make an excuse that you have to get home early from work.

- You generally have to shave the back of your own neck between haircuts.

- No one is there when you finally win at solitaire.

- When you run into friends at the grocery store, you can't pretend that all that junk food in the cart isn't for you.

- Being in an Internet chat room isn't really having a social life.

- You have to wear a long raincoat to church on a summer day to have a friend there zip your dress.

- It's virtually impossible to put a bed frame together by yourself.

- You have no one else to blame when you're late.

- Putting the Christmas lights on the tree can become a prickly situation.

- When can I ignore that strange smell, and when do I need to get out of the house?

- You don't have to wait until you blow two head gaskets to understand the meaning of the words: oil change.

- Sitting next to that man with a strange smell at the airport terminal, you wish you had someone to pick you up at 2:00 A.M.

- How do you get that mustard stain out? How do you sew on a button, anyway?

- Heimlich for one just can't be easy.

based on his *7 Habits of Highly Effective People.* His challenge is to "begin with the end in mind." What do I want my friends and family to say about me when I am gone? What do I want to hear Jesus say when I am at the pearly gates? When I am planning my schedule, I should mark out time and tasks that support these goals first. I should look at each role I play in my life and what my goals are, then mark my calendar. If I don't take this approach, I get buried with the urgent tasks in my life rather than the important tasks. Time is my most precious asset at this point in my life. I want to be a good steward of it.

Nathan—I was in a session about developing ministry teams for singles, and we were asked to give common descriptors about singles. "Fun-loving" was hollered first, then a long pause. "Non-committal" was offered up and then "career-oriented." Finally a woman groaned, "Possessing a lot of time." I could tell from her tone that most people believe that she, being single, had plenty of it and made requests of her freely. Everyone groaned a little to affirm her suffering.

The night before I accepted the writing assignment for time management for this book, I stated myself that singles have more time than most people and should get it together and accomplish more. There I was being duplicitous. The truth be known, I'm as busy as anyone else, and yes, I believe a lot of people perceive us to be "the bored single" looking for something to fill up the time.

I had also moaned the night of the writing assignments about my own insurmountable schedule: I was embarking—continually embarking—on another task. There is the project at work, which nobody else assumes, of cleaning up the abhorrent network. So I was to tackle it and become the network hero. There are these fine art paintings that I should knock out—just for my own good. There are the illustrative commercial/editorial paintings that my portfolio is lacking. There are all of the illustrations for children's literature that I haven't even begun planning—a sad thing, since this is where I really want my career to go. There, of course, is this book—a noble undertaking.

Do singles have more time at their disposal than most people? In my case, as with all my friends, there aren't any children who need to play ball before dinner, or PTA, or problems with their schooling. There isn't that spouse character needing help with the dishes; in fact, the dishes can go sour for days in the sink with no one complaining. It seems that we should have time. Still, everyone I know is burning the candle hard and fast at both ends. Singles must need to take on more than they can handle to justify themselves in their churches, communities, and jobs. Maybe we are securing relationships by making sure that a lot of people need us. Maybe we just can't say "no."

I am learning that life is a short jaunt. The days that have gone by and the amount of things I am trying to accomplish have helped me learn that I will have to choose a few things to do well or risk becoming mediocre at a million things. Jesus said, "So, because you are lukewarm—neither hot nor cold—I am about to spit you out of my mouth" (Revelation 3:16). These words, though referring to the fervor of our individual faith, can also apply well to the way we conquer the vocations and avocations of our lives.

An art instructor in college made me write my goals for the next five years and, moreover, my strategy and tactics for meeting them. It was studio art class, and we were being pounded with goal planning. It was painful and seemed absurd, but I had to do it anyway. I had no idea. I just wanted to be great. How on earth is a twenty-one-year-old idealist sitting cross-legged in a gallery supposed to set up goals for life like bowling pins to be knocked down? We were to be very specific. How? I could barely get through fifty hand-thrown pots, a government class essay, five large airbrush paintings, several etchings, lithos, and block-prints, and many small tests and quizzes during an average semester. I could not imagine getting a career as an artist when I thought of it being even busier and more important than all of that. How could I say that I would be an art director at NBC within five years when I didn't even know how to write a résumé? This moody artist-in-residence drove home the fact that goal planning was the fire for the forge if I wanted to go anywhere.

No, I never became an art director at NBC, nor do I have a notion to do so. But when you are in college, you have to aim high. And anything big like that seems cool. I have worked in a fast-paced book design market for several years now. I refer to it as working at the fast-food window at McDonald's, but in a corporate office and designing books projected to net a million or more, instead of pushing fries. It's just as fast, just as hectic, just as boggling. I can't imagine doing anything bigger, faster, or cheesier (like television). So my goals have changed.

We need to do our goal planning. It's nearly a daylong task. It feels foolish when I'm in the midst of it, but it helps keep me closer to a target, especially when I have the goals written down with a few steps plotted throughout my year's calendar. I know my odds of getting "there" are slim if I don't have a clear view of where I want to be in five years.

We are accountable to God. Every task or favor someone presents us is arguably valuable, worthy, and needed. We, however, have been given only so many days and have also been given the responsibility to strive with God to fulfill His purpose in our lives. We must make a choice among a few things and make them precious gifts to give back to Him.

Dana—I want every second to count. I want to make the most of every situation. I know that this is the day that the Lord has made—but where did He put all my hours? Too often I find myself wishing for more time. I want to be more organized; I want to feel together on the inside. But I let time control me. It seems to close in on me and slip away with no warning.

A lot of my time mismanagement has to do with my hectic schedule. As many singles do, I pack everything possible into my day, thinking I am being proactive and efficient, but I often end up exhausted and only 75 percent effective. I actually like keeping busy, serving, and being involved. I just wish I had innate time management cells pulsating throughout my body. I have the big, hefty planner and try to utilize my communication skills to avoid unnecessary meetings, but everything just seems to take longer than I expected. Maybe when I am eighty years old, I will have some sense of the time needed to complete a task effectively. Often my tendencies toward perfection seem to hinder setting and reaching my goals. I never want to settle for less than my best, but because I haven't quite figured out how to achieve certain things in a given amount of time, I am often left frustrated with my good intentions. I want desperately for people to know they can count on me. I'm learning a lot about God's grace.

Other Voices

Heather Floyd, Point of Grace—*Time. It's so easy to waste it. I could look back at the end of a day and say I could have accomplished so much more than I did. But I wasted an hour watching Rosie. I have to watch Rosie.*

Rebecca St. James—*Sometimes it's quite overwhelming trying to juggle friendships and working on an album and being out on the road and church time, quiet time, interviews, working on books—everything—but my dad really helps me with time management. He's my manager, so he makes sure that I'm not being overwhelmed with too much stuff.*

Max Hsu, Church of Rhythm—I'm not a big fan of "You have all the time on the planet when you're single." It's like I can twiddle my thumbs all by myself now.

Vacations
"I'll just buy a change of clothes on the way out of town."

Chris—The best three things about teaching: June, July, and August.

If Lisa wants to take a week off and go to Colorado, I'm there. And someone from the singles' group is getting up a five-day houseboat trip. Let's see. Yep. I can make it. And I hear there's a three-day Christian concert festival a few states over. All I need is someone to go with, and we're there. I may not even pack; maybe I'll just buy a fresh change of clothes on my way out of town.

Because I have a great network of friends in my singles' group at church, I don't find it too difficult to find traveling companions.

I couldn't travel alone, though. A friend of mine planned a week in Costa Rica, snorkeling, scuba diving, rafting, and more. He was going to do this all alone, even with minimal Spanish knowledge. On tour the first day, he met a couple of guys who invited him to join them the next day, and the next. He even went on a high-class white-water rafting expedition with some of the guides he met on a lower-class river. Though he nearly drowned, he had a great time. He planned this vacation to be alone. He wanted to go alone.

Last summer thirteen of us rented a seventy-five-foot houseboat on Dale Hollow Lake on the Kentucky-Tennessee border. For four days we swam, water-skied, jet-skied, watched videos, played cards, and hiked. We took turns leading devotions in the morning and the evening. Even though I was on vacation, I treasured the devotion times. We shared our hearts. We prayed. We encouraged each other, like only Christian brothers and sisters could.

One afternoon, we took turns reading our favorite psalms out loud on top of the houseboat. As we shared why the psalm meant so much to us, we shared a part of our lives. We read with passion and emphasis the words God had for us during our times of trial or rejoicing.

It was a great trip. It didn't take a lot of planning. We just rented the boat and bought food. And I got to drive the speedboat as much as I wanted.

Nathan—I don't write this from the standpoint of always being content. When I think about my job and that I am self-sufficient—that I can take off on a weekend when I want to, that I set any course for myself without consulting others on every decision—I realize what a gift of independence I have. I think about things like learning Italian, becoming a better artist, and traveling to places that most people don't think of: visiting Portugal, walking through Wales, or seeing the oldest church in Christendom. I am reaching a point where saving for trips is becoming a priority. It's important to experience the world. I haven't felt myself fretting about who to go with; maybe I'll go alone and group up with people on a train. I think that going with travel groups is a great way to network friendships around the country. This just gives you more places to go.

Maybe short-term mission trips are a consideration. Maybe I'll visit some people whom I have been supporting. I think that contentment as a single is very centered on spending time doing valuable things. Working in the inner city or donating time to organizations that need me are on my list of things to do. I know I can't stew about my own worries when I am busy helping someone else out of a jam. It totally takes the focus off of me.

Dana—I think it's important to consider any opportunity to get away. But as a single adult, I choose not to travel alone. I think it's a great idea to get a group of people together for the weekend and take off for some R&R. It seems, though, that up until the last few years my vacations only included family members. However, a couple of summers ago a white-water rafting trip broke that pattern. About eighteen people from church braved the rapids, and some of us went camping as well. It was pretty funny to witness everyone's tent-building techniques and approaches to successful camping.

Last summer my friend Carla and I went to Estes Park, Colorado, to attend the Christian Artists seminar. It was exciting traveling together—just the two of us—and very comical. Two gals with no real sense of direction should never be left alone with a map, no strict time restrictions, and a rental car. We enjoyed the seminar but spent the majority of our time navigating the narrow winding roads along the Rocky Mountains. Did I mention that Carla is afraid of heights? Yes, the driver in control admitted she had no business behind the wheel, but I wasn't about to volunteer. What an excursion. We planned out the entire trip and enjoyed the freedom to roam.

Since I have no instant traveling companion, it's nice to have an available group of friends to vacation with. Another large group of us from church, some married, most single, went on a houseboat trip in Dale Hollow, Tennessee. Pauley, whom I consider the master of all vacation planners, organized the trip down to the very last detail. We tied two houseboats together and docked in a cove for the weekend. While I mostly took advantage of the rafts and rays, others tackled watersports that required much more coordination. We shared three speedboats and various water skis, wake boards, and other equipment. When we were not out on the water, there were tons of snacks to munch on and spontaneous challenges (such as turning flips off the side of the boat or the no-handed applesauce eating contest) to keep us occupied or entertained. A group of four or five different people was responsible for food preparation and cleanup for one meal a day during the holiday weekend. Dinner was my favorite meal, as we all gathered on one boat to pray together and bless the food. Afterward we would sit back and recap the day. I would retreat to the top of the boat, lie on a spare sleeping bag, and stare upward into the massive cluster of stars in the dark sky. I had no consideration of time. My mind was clear of hectic schedules, the daily routine back home. It was great just hanging out.

Lana—Two of the best benefits of being single are having more discretionary income and more time than our married counterparts. Last summer I traveled to Australia with a friend. I was surprised that several singles joined our tour and came alone. I was impressed with their courage to travel across the world with strangers. I don't think I could. However, singles sometimes have a hard time finding others to travel with.

One singles' ministry in Ohio helps plan vacations for their singles. They'll take a one-week vacation with almost thirty of the members. Our singles' ministry also plans several mission trips each year. We'll take three days of vacation to go work harder than we would at our present jobs.

I don't usually have a problem finding someone to go on vacation; it's the money to go on vacation that's more challenging. It isn't until recently that I finally got on the other side of paying off some business debts. Now I can see the light and want to travel more.

Other Voices

Mark Lowry, Out of Control—*A few years back, my brother had the great idea for our family to take a skiing vacation. . . . I leased some skis, and I borrowed a ski suit from a fat friend of mine. I looked like the Pillsbury Doughboy in a Hefty bag. When we hit the slopes, I asked my brother, "Where do I take skiing lessons?"*

He said "Skiing lessons? Mark, you don't need skiing lessons. Haven't you seen the skiers on TV? You just get out there and keep your balance and head down the hill as fast as you can go.". . . My brother pushed me—way before I was ready. . . . I was flying past other skiers, wimps taking their time swishing from side to side down the hill, screaming all the way down.

When I finally got to the bottom of the hill, I started looking for the brakes. That's when I realized I had forgotten to ask my brother that important question. Where were the brakes on skis? Then I found out. The brakes were the people right in front of me, standing in the ski-lift line. "Excuse Me" (Wham!!), "Pardon me" (Slam!!), "Coming through!" (Pow! Whack! Thud!).

I lay there in a big pile of wet snow with the breath knocked out of me, my ribs cracked, my poles and skis pointing every direction but right, wishing I was on the beaches of Hawaii, getting a good, ordinary, third-degree sunburn.[1]

Mark Wesner, Singles Minister—*One thing that's necessary in order to take a vacation is what some financial experts call "discretionary income." I'd have to say that, when I was single, I remember actually having some of that! Now our standard vacation plan is the "mooch off the friends and relatives" travel package.*

Off the Clock
"I need some downtime."

Lana—Two books that I have never finished are *When I Relax, I Feel Guilty* and *Too Busy Not to Pray.* Unfortunately, both books also describe my life. I have a difficult time vegging out. I sometimes feel guilty if I am not being productive. My prayer life also reflects that. I'm trying to make sure I spend plenty of time with God but often the visible, tangible to-dos steal my attention away from the patient, loving God who would like to spend time with me.

Bill Hybels from Willow Creek Community Church really convicted me in his message about our need to have time to unwind. When I look at my life, it is easy to read most of the gauges. The physical gauge: Am I eating right and exercising? The spiritual gauge: Am I spending time with God? The mental gauge: Am I being challenged mentally? The emotional gauge is often neglected. This gauge is more difficult to measure: Are my emotional batteries charged up? Do I participate in activities where I can relax and get my mind off life? Some great activities for this are golfing, reading a good book, fishing, or floating in a raft. For me, it's reading or riding my bike.

However, is reading or biking what takes up my time when I am alone? I can't say so. This time is split primarily in two areas: church activities and my computer. I try to be in a Bible study that requires me to be in the Word daily. I need the discipline. I am also active in our singles' group and have been in several leadership positions.

My computer is my baby. I'm not happy if my computer isn't working. I enjoy being creative on my PC. For example, this Christmas I created personalized Christmas cards, a calendar for my family, and a picture celebrating my parents' fortieth anniversary. I use my PC for everything. I do my finances in Quicken, keep track of my workouts in Access, and am also doing my family's genealogy, including scanning in pictures.

With my other spare time, I love being with people: going to movies, biking, eating out or playing cards or board games. I am a mean card player. I like cribbage, hearts, and, of course, euchre. In Indiana, you have to play euchre or you're not a true Hoosier.

Dana—To everything there is a season. And to every day, I could handle having nothing but spare time. Too often, I'm grasping for minutes here and there just to sit down and relax. I'm searching for time to do special things for others. And I'm longing for time to be still. I've been praying for more discipline and quality time with the Lord. Apart from that, I desperately want time to organize my life and to work toward specific long-term goals.

If I were only concerned with utilizing spare moments, paying the bills would be much more tolerable. How wonderful it would be to read all the books I have accumulated that are nicely arranged but collecting dust on my shelf! I would fill my days writing in my journal, learning and singing new songs, or even working on original music arrangements. And maybe those deep, hidden desires of mine to cook and clean would surface. I'd love to invite my friends over to my well-kept place for dinner and relaxed conversation. I'm always up for swimming, boating, or lying out by the water. If given the time, I'd talk more, sleep more, take more spontaneous weekend road trips, watch a Broadway play, eat lots of popcorn, take a picnic basket and blanket to the outdoor symphony concert, or go shopping and actually buy something.

Though it would be nice to commit all my days to fun-things-that-Dana-likes-to-do, obviously, the demands of daily living squelch my spare time. But as a single gal, I do seem to have more time available, or I'm often able to be a bit more flexible than others are. When this is the case, I want to be wise with that time and take advantage of opportunities to do for others. I find so much joy in serving and spending time with people; I want to know what they are all about and what makes them get up in the morning.

I have come to the realization that no one really has time, that we all have to make time for things that are important to us. A friend of mine once said of herself, "I am the busiest person I know." She then laughed and said, "I realize it doesn't make much sense to claim that, when everyone else I know is saying the same thing." How true. I was convicted.

God gave all of us twenty-four hours in the day.

Chris—God is life, the rest is volleyball. I love playing. There's a lot of instant gratification going on. The 6'8" big guy slams the ball I set him, then slaps my hand with a verbal, "Nice set." Or he nods in affirmation. Or he points at me as if to say, "It's all you, it's all you."

It's enough to keep me coming back. Right now, I play a lot with a group I met through league play a few years ago. Only a few are Christians, and, while they are good sports, you can certainly tell that they are not walking with God. We try to play a couple of hours every Saturday. Sometimes I live for it because I don't allow for much in the physical realm on my weekly calendar.

I have always been a team player. I was voted most athletic girl of my senior class, and I played most of the sports in high school. I continue to enjoy volleyball and softball, but, as my body easily testifies, I haven't had a coach make me run suicides in quite a while.

I also enjoy photography and writing. I love to write my

prayers to God—it helps me to focus. I often rewrite psalms, hymns, or songs to reflect my day.

Other Voices

Geof Barkley—*Spare time. This is where singleness really shows.*

I am into computers. I do one-D design; it is all straight lines. I enjoy basketball and college football, so when those two seasons roll around, I try to spend my time doing that. And I also enjoy interior design.

Heather Floyd, Point of Grace—*I work out, take a photography class and guitar lessons. I don't have much free time, and we're working on finalizing the album, sometimes till 11:00 or 12:00 at night.*

Gary Mullet—*I'm currently in my third childhood. I am into computers, books, and remote-controlled airplanes. I've built a lot of airplanes and stuff. So, my house looks like a giant shop. I get all the stuff I wish I could have had as a kid.*

Michael Passons, Avalon—*I like photography. I take my camera with me, but I don't do all my little artsy stuff because everyone complains, "All you take are pictures of birds and flowers." There is also a lot of stuff that comes around Nashville like arts festivals and flea markets. I love to go to that kind of stuff. I love movies and, of course, Rio Bravo, our favorite restaurant. We sit on the patio. That's the greatest, just hanging out with friends.*

Max Hsu, Church of Rhythm—*I don't tend to do things in my spare time; I tend to try things. I try to do two new things a season. This season I've got one down. I've learned to ride horses for real. Last season was snowboarding and snowmobiling. The season before that was skydiving and a list of things. I used to play paintball and do lots of rock climbing. I've tried almost everything you can think of.*

Rebecca St. James—*I love being at home with my family. I love getting outside and mowing the lawn, or lately it's been gardening. I'd like to do a bit more of that.*

Jaci Velasquez—*I usually don't have spare time when I am traveling, but, when I am home, I have a lot of spare time. When I am home, I like to go downtown and hang out at coffee shops, eat a lot, go shopping, and do all the things I love to do—like rock climbing.*

Pam Thum—*I love hiking and four-wheeling. My favorite thing to do in the whole world is horseback riding. And writing: I'm working on a movie right now with a friend of mine.*

Serving in Church
"I feel normal at my church."

Dana—Unfortunately, I think some feel that our singles' ministry has a reputation of being one of the biggest pickup places for Christian singles. How disappointing that some choose to reduce such a dynamic ministry to a dating pool. My motivation for attending has been for spiritual and emotional healing and for a deeper understanding of the Word. This church has become my church home and a place for me to grow while sharing in my single life. It provides an opportunity to fellowship with those with whom I can relate. Sure, I can be in danger of getting too comfortable in my own little world of thriving singles, but I always pray that God will make me sensitive to this danger and that I will continue to grow.

I am so thankful my church acknowledges that singles are unmarried adults and not social misfits who have missed the boat, or who are not complete, or who are in a holding tank.

Too often, it seems that churches mean well, but they don't make room for singles. I think it can be easy for these churches to assume they can nurture singles by squeezing them into any group. We are just as in need of personal and applicable teaching as the husband, wife, child, or elder. The Church has to focus on providing opportunities for all of the Body to serve and grow and not on shuffling around its unmarried members until they "graduate."

Nathan—When I went looking for a church, I admit, I gravitated to one that had an active singles' ministry. I'm torn whether or not that was the right thing to do. I was new to the community and wanted to connect with people who were like me. I think that was okay for the search for friendship. I wanted single, Christian friends, so I went to where I could find them.

I think the purpose of the Church is to equip God's people to go out and be salt and light, and ours certainly does a good job of this. I admit that part of the reason for my choosing my church was its size, its ability to offer *me* a lot. There's every style of music, activity, and group. But I must also give to the church and then leave its walls to reach out to the world. I haven't given everything I should. When I finish this book, I promise to look for where I can give more.

Chris—I'm probably one of the few Christians who will admit a struggle with church. I just don't have that strong desire to get there every week.

The Church today is so far from what it seems Christ meant when He told Peter that he was the rock on which He'd build

His church. Sometimes I think that God isn't all that pleased when He sees His children congregate to listen to some guy speak. He wanted a place for people to feel accepted, be nourished, be reminded of His grace and love, and be convicted to live out their commitment to Him. Did they have pews in the Acts church? Did they have that part in the service where everyone had to greet those next to them? Did they quickly shake hands with and smile at their three-person quota and then sit down, or did they embrace one another and stop to listen and care? Did they have special music? Was the service always so predictable? Did they dress up so much? Were they in a hurry to leave? Did they get angry if the preacher went over by ten minutes? What ever happened to "they had all things in common"?

Rather than complain about what the church isn't, or add to the problem, I should work to improve it. We are the ones who are pew-sitting spectators rather than participants in what God wants for us inside His sanctuary and in His world.

Even with my struggles with my own church, I know that I need to be there. Though once in a while I will stay home to spend alone time with God, I also need to be with people, to see Jesus in their faces and actions, and to minister alongside them.

Singles need the Church because everyone has a need to be needed, and the Church needs us. We do have more flexible time, and we do seem to be the younger, more energetic types. The acceptance and responsibility can build us up, and we can build the Body by giving back in vision and in action.

As a single I don't feel less accepted than others are in the Church. A recently married friend who was searching for a new church observed that friendly church people approach singles more often. She said that she and her husband would walk in and sit down—rarely did someone talk to them any more than a greeting, and never did anyone offer to sit with them. On the other hand, she watched as solo visitors would have conversations with church members, and they would find a seat together. She speculates that someone sitting by himself is an open invitation for friendship; seeing someone alone challenges members to action, while a couple may not seem to need befriending. After all, they have each other.

Lana—I attend a large church that sincerely strives to be a suitable Bride of Christ. It has its problems, as all churches do, but it's open to all types of people. As a single, I feel accepted and valued. Most importantly, I feel normal! But even with a large singles' ministry and a very accepting attitude toward non-marrieds, it occasionally slips into thinking that singles aren't truly adults. As the church network administrator, one of my responsibilities was keeping the church's summary attendance statistics. I was blown away when I discovered that our Sunday school class for singles was not included in the total for adult Bible school. We were just an older youth group! I changed that, then and there.

Some churches are even less single-sensitive. I heard of one church that had a Sunday school class called "Pairs and Spares." What single would want to go there?

Going to church is important to me. I don't feel good if I don't go. It's part of my witness. I also try not to focus on what I get out of it. Worship shouldn't be something we rate like a movie but something we do. Worship is a verb. And church is far more than somewhere we go; it's who we are. We are our part of God's Church.

I love that our church has a large singles' population. There's always something to do and people to meet. But I need to see marrieds and children too. They keep me balanced. I am so thankful for the many couples that encourage me weekly: the

Bundys, the Warners, the Jonsons, and others who live out their Christian lives. If I ever get married, these couples have given me godly examples to follow.

Church is where I serve. Our church really encourages its members to learn their spiritual gifts and strive to use them. When I've indicated an interest in an area, our church has given me the freedom and opportunity to run with it.

This church is also where I've met my closest friends, and it's my haven when I'm hurting. When I lost my dream job, my church was there to help me work through my issues. Our church continues to point me to Jesus and to becoming a better me. I don't know what my life would be without it.

Other Voices

Benji Gaither, Benjamin—The church's job isn't to fix me up.

Rich Vincent, Singles Minister—There are a couple of things I think a single ought to look for; I'm not necessarily convinced that singles should look for a singles' ministry, but I am convinced they should look for a church that is going to embrace them and not be so family-oriented that the single feels neglected. It means the church needs to be aware that a high percentage of the population is single and that it can't just keep having "Marriage and Family" things unless they're going to talk about the singles. We would absolutely turn Paul and Jesus away from the door if we kept talking about marriage and family so much.

Ministry
"At work, at home, or at church"

Dana—I equate ministry with my passions in life, utilizing my gifts for God's glory. When I think of all the ways He has blessed my life, I can't help but want to serve Him, to give thanks to Him, to come alongside and work with Him.

Music is my passion in life; it brings me so much joy. When I sing, I feel like I am praying to Him, for who He is and for His sacrifice. The Lord has blessed us with so many unique gifts and abilities that I think it should be our greatest desire to want to discover and use those gifts in ministry for Him. Music is most fulfilling to me when I know I have touched someone through it. I have been singing as far back as I can remember and have always enjoyed it, but I have come to realize that it doesn't mean as much until God uses it for His purpose. I want God to use the lyrics of a song to speak through me. I am now involved in a vocal group in our singles' ministry, and we sing at local churches and events. We love to sing, but we're finding out how challenging it is to be involved in a group with four dominant female personalities. We are in constant prayer as to how God would have us to act and to respond to one another. Though it has its difficult aspects, the best part about our group is the fellowship—we just love being around each other, and we love singing together. Apart from that, we are trusting the Lord to guide our ministry together. We just want to be open to His leading and His purpose for our music. He may call us to serve in a different way; whatever the case, we're just constantly going to be singing and praising Him.

Nathan—I believe that ministry is the way I live my life in accordance with the truth God has shown me. I think it's day in and day out, the way I relate to the people around me at work and show them the love of God. I fall down in this all the time. I don't necessarily believe in speaking a testimony to people all the time but in being ready to stand for what we believe in word and deed when the rubber meets the road.

When I talk disparagingly about other people, even when it's true, I cause others to lower their opinions of that person. When I complain about my job, I drag others down; when I don't stand up for my beliefs when they are attacked verbally, I deny God His glory; and when I don't speak clearly about my faith when directly asked, I betray the Lord. This must be the toughest thing we have to go through as Christians in America, but it is laughable compared to what Christians around the world must suffer for their faith.

As singles, I think we have been given an opportunity to perform an extra measure of ministry. I was going to help hand out gloves and coats downtown during the Advent season, but, of course, I got tied up in my Christmas shopping and Christmas dinners. Throughout the summer, our church gives us opportunities to do things like hand out free Cokes at sporting events to illustrate Christ's love in a simple and significant way, but I just haven't taken the opportunity. I need to block these things into my schedule. I do not have the same responsibilities right now that married people do; I should be able to give a little more. I also think that this is the best time to establish a habit of extra ministry, so if I do marry, it will already be part of my life.

First, I must pray for fortitude during my daily ministry, then I must pray for motivation to establish that extra measure of ministry that God has blessed me to do in the time that I am single.

Chris—Taking a spiritual gift test really helped me understand where I should focus my energy in ministry. Once we figure out what gifts God has given us, we can better serve Him and be happier serving Him. God's will for us is revealed in our gifts.

The test showed that my highest gift is in apostleship, which means I enjoy starting new programs, like a visionary. I also scored high in administration, wisdom, and teaching.

I believe that we also have God-given passions for certain people groups or areas of ministry. I have a passion for teenagers. I want to help them make right life decisions. So I will be my happiest when working with teens on a new project, which I guess is why I like taking them to Mexico each summer to build a house or enjoy planning each week's Campus Life meeting with the student leaders.

Even though I have gifts that are more action-oriented and scored pretty low in emotion-based areas like mercy or giving, I know that God wants me to balance my work with my love for Him and His people.

We are ministers wherever we are—at work, at home, or at church. We are doing ministry every waking second. We have the opportunity to make those seconds count for the Kingdom.

Lana—I worked full-time at our church for more than two years as their network administrator, responsible for all the computers at church. It was a great experience, but I prefer being involved as a layperson or volunteer. Sometimes it is good not to know everything that goes on. It can be good to be at a distance and not be so familiar with church issues. I also got very tired of that building because I was there six days a week. And, of course, now in the corporate world, the money is better. I didn't leave for any of those reasons. I just knew it was time to move on.

Ever since high school, I've been involved in church activities. I don't even think about it. It's what I do. However, in the last few years I have learned the importance of understanding my spiritual gifts and finding the best, most fulfilling place to serve. For example, I have the gift of administration, and I definitely don't have the gift of mercy. I certainly would do better at organizing an upcoming concert than volunteering at a shelter. However, God still calls me to be merciful and to help the poor and, sometimes, to be stretched and willing to go outside of my comfort zone. The key is understanding how I was created and being obedient in doing what God has called me to do.

Other Voices

Pam Thum—As I sat in a quaint bookstore/coffee bar, a girl who had heard my music asked me why I believed in Jesus and told me how she was hurting. I got to share the love and truth of Jesus with her and pray with her.

Cherie Paliotta, Avalon—I am finding so much fulfillment serving the Lord in the venue that He has provided. . . . When I am on that platform and I see people raising their hands and coming to the Lord, getting saved and delivered, that's what it's all about.

Rebecca St. James—My pastor last week talked about making wise decisions in life. He said to ask God for wisdom. It was based on James 1. He was saying that in the ministry, but it's really the same in whatever calling you have in life. He'll ask God for wisdom up to fifty times a day. Right before he's gonna call someone or talk to somebody or while he's preparing his sermon or just for day-to-day things, he'll just say, "God, give me wisdom." I've noticed myself, since he said that, doing that. In making decisions, ask for wisdom.

Rich Mullins—Singleness is irrelevant to my ministry. It's kind of like saying that having brown eyes or blue eyes is better. It's just nice to have eyes. Lots of people get by without them.

3

Not Yet Promoted to the Grown-Up Table

(Awkward Situations)

I walked into the doctor's office. My head had been plugged up for three weeks straight. *I must have a sinus infection; I need drugs*, I thought. I stood at the receptionist's counter with a closed window in my face, trying not to stare at the frenzied receptionist, waiting patiently through pressure and pain for her to acknowledge me in my suffering.

Finally, she flung the window aside. "Yes?"

"Nathan Clement to see the doctor at 10:00," I honked. She shuffled charts and looked annoyed. "I don't have you on the schedule, but I do have your wife. Did you switch and not notify our office?"

"Huh?"

"Yes, I have a Mrs. Clement down but not you."

"You mean my mom?"

"No, I'm sure your wife."

"I don't have a wife," I retorted. At this she flung a chart open and displayed the contents to me, which contained a photograph clipped on the inside cover.

"Then who's this?" She pointed defiantly at the picture.

"That's me!" The picture was at least seventeen years old. I was in the seventh grade when it was taken. Okay, so it was the seventies and my hair hung down to my eyes and over my ears and I had a smooth oval face. But I was certain it wasn't my wife. Even though my head was a ticking time bomb, I was certain I didn't have a wife and was appalled that I actually had to try to convince her.

She distractedly told me to get a new snapshot taken before I left the office, as if it were my fault.

Ordinary situations can easily become awkward and even emotionally draining for singles. Sitting in a pew, watching your third friend this summer get married, you wish you could get your hands on the magic potion they're all using. And what's up with that question, "When are you going to get married?" Like you can just look up the date in your day planner. What kind of an answer are people expecting?

A lot of singles have family pressure, which doesn't make it easier to be (or even pretend to be) content. And knowing that your class reunion is coming up doesn't help. Learn to laugh at the situation and choose to develop your character. The situation above was always a little bit painful, but by writing about it, I was able to laugh at it and realize it was no biggie.

Family Expectations
"So, are you seeing anyone right now?"

Chris—My aunt asked way too often why I wasn't married. As she got older and her sharp mind became dull, she would ask me in the most inappropriate situations why I didn't have someone. One time, at a baby shower, in front of all the women in my family, she again sighed at me. "Dear, you still don't have anyone? *You do like boys, don't you?*"

So now when I see her and her failing little mind, and she asks me about my social life, I want to respond, "I told you that

I've been married for two years. Don't you remember seeing Jim and the baby at Christmas?"

Often I'd be talking to Mom on the phone and I'd hear Dad, joking, say, "Ask her if she's married yet." When I was in college, he'd say it so often that one time, when I was frustrated, I told him that I wouldn't visit anymore if he kept bothering me. He stopped for a while and Mom got on him about what he did say.

They just want me to be happy. But why does the world see marriage as "happy" when more than 50 percent end in a devastating divorce? Though we don't have an abundance of divorces in my family tree, we don't exactly have the happily-ever-after stories either.

When my parents talk about my life, they use words like "social butterfly" to describe how active I am, and I never, ever share regrets about not having anyone in my life . . . nothing to give them the impression that I'm not happy with my life. I *am* happy with my life. So why do I need to be fixed?

555 Singles Surveyed

Does Your Family Treat You Differently
Because You Are Single?

Most of the Time 9%
Some of the Time 39%
Never 52%

Dana—Since I am the younger of two children, I have been and probably always will be seen by Mom and Dad as their "little girl." I have wonderful parents, and, as I have gotten older, I am thankful that they have never pressured me to date or marry. I know that they have always wanted the best for me.

However, as my single years unfold, they continue to be somewhat protective. It seems my singleness dictates their perception of me; sometimes it's difficult to share a decision with them without hearing how they would handle it. As a parent, I'm sure it's not so easy knowing how much space to give and when to step in, but I can't help feeling that if I were already married, my parents would naturally realize my independence from them as well as my desire to work with my spouse to handle situations. I want my family to be involved in my life; I just don't want them to feel like they must intervene and carry my burdens or stress. They have taught me well how to handle life, and I would like nothing more than to do that, free from too much parental concern or worry.

Maybe we just need to hang out more. And one thing I would like to offer them is my presence (after twenty-eight years) at the grown-up table during family gatherings. I could actually dine next to the parents and other deserving adults. Meanwhile, I'm getting used to the hard folding chairs at the covered card table. At least it's familiar. I've grown rather fond of my mismatched place setting, complete with paper napkins.

Nathan—I think my family worries about me. My mom worries that I'm eating right and eating enough. She makes sure everyone eats well, including those who don't even live with her. Mom seals part of every meal in those plastic containers—some of them go off to my grandma for microwave meals, and some are saved for me to pick up when I go home to visit. It makes it easier, knowing there are several containers in the freezer and I can coast until the next paycheck.

I think they also worry about my having someone. They've never wanted me to let that someone get away. "When are you going to ask that woman to marry you?" my mom asked frankly one day. "Mom!" I protested. "It's our business." And that was that. She apologized, but she didn't have to. It's her job to make sure I don't miss what's right in front of me. I should have apologized for being so sharp.

My aunt knows all about being single, but since she has found her perfect man (my junior high principal, of all people!), she can't help but fix up everyone else so they, too, can experience the marital bliss she has. She has always been more of a chum than an aunt or parental figure. She was single for a long time, was a big Evie fan, went to "Jesus '77," wore bell-bottoms with daisy prints, and had a lot of fun. She would offer good advice when my dating wasn't going well or when I just got dumped. She would say, "Well, she's obviously not what you want, since she can't see how perfect you are." She would always be a shot in the arm as well as a testimony to me that living single can be fun and victorious.

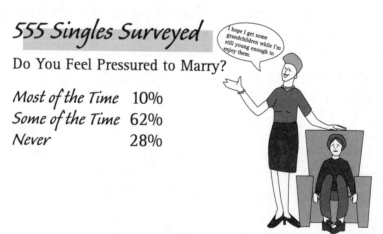

555 Singles Surveyed

I hope I get some grandchildren while I'm still young enough to enjoy them.

Do You Feel Pressured to Marry?

Most of the Time	10%
Some of the Time	62%
Never	28%

Lana—In my family, the best benefit of being single is that I'm only asked to bring the rolls or soda for family pitch-ins. Once I'm married, I'll be expected to cook a real dish.

Going to family reunions is never much fun for me as a single adult. "Why aren't you married?" I get asked again and again.

"Because I always kill my boyfriends after the third date." What am I supposed to say?

Recently another relative asked about a guy I was dating: "What's wrong with him that he's thirty-six and never been married?" I replied, "What's wrong with me? I'm thirty-five and have never married." "Oh, there's nothing wrong with you," she said, but it makes me wonder.

When asked why I don't have a date for a family function or wedding, my favorite response is, "All my boyfriends like to spend Friday nights with their wives." I like going for the shock value.

Other Voices

Max Hsu, Church of Rhythm—*My grandfather is very culturally Chinese. He sat down with me at my brother's wedding and said, "Are you seeing anyone?" And I said not really. He said, "Well, you should get married," and I told him that I agreed with him in principle. He was like, "Why don't you get married by Thanksgiving?" And this was in August. I told him that it's not quite as simple as it was in the old days. He gave me a longer grace period after a little pressure.*

Mark Lowry, Out of Control—*According to my friends, I just can't LIVE without that ring on my finger.*

But you know what?

Jesus was single.

So when people say, "When are you going to get married?" I say, "Listen, every time you pray, you're praying to a single adult, and don't you forget it."[1]

Pam Thum—*I can be number one for five weeks and [my parents are] happy for me, but they still say, "But we want you to get married." "Mother, I know that, but you don't want me to get married to the wrong one, do you?" She knows that. She'll just be very happy. She'll take a deep sigh.*

Gary Mullet—*If I go out on a date, everybody is always immediately asking, "So how did it go? How did it go?" I've had this kind of casual dating relationship just recently. In fact, the whole family keeps their ears to the ground. They've never called me as much: "So how is she? How is she doing?" But the whole relationship is tapering off a little bit—you know, we are both really busy right now. So I'll talk to them, and they'll say, "So how is she?" "Well, you know we are both kind of losing a little bit of interest, just kind of waning a little bit." "Oh really, what happened? We just thought she was the one."*

Reasons to Explain Why You're Not Married:

- I'm hooked on Campbell's "Meals for One."

- I have traditional nonfamily values.

- I can't find anyone who organizes his/her music collection or kitchen the way I do.

- I just don't have the energy to have the relationship thing.

- When you marry, you become boring. . . . Uh, not that you're boring. . . . I'm speaking in generalities, and you're certainly the exception to the rule.

- It makes *Seinfeld* (or *Friends*) funnier.

- How will my single friends get a ride to the airport if I marry?

- Someone's got to live in these teeny apartments.

- I just don't like the idea of getting all dressed up for a wedding.

- Why would I want to ruin my décor with a houseful of crummy brass candlesticks given as wedding presents?

Taken from Michael Nolan and Eve Sarrett, *I'm So Tired of Other People, I'm Dating Myself* (Nashville, Tenn.: Thomas Nelson Publishers, 1993).

Not Yet Promoted to the Grown-Up Table

They always express interest, but at the same time we've seen a lot of close family members and people around us have a lot of trouble and make bad decisions about marriage or how to handle it once they are married. And I am not in a hurry. And Mom and Dad have been great about that. They know I'm waiting and trying to play it correctly.

Jody McBrayer, Avalon—When I moved to Nashville, my mom came and did all the decorating and stuff; she loves to do that. The only time I get frustrated is when I bring someone home who I am dating. My parents love everybody. They never say, "Oh, I don't like her very much." They always say, "Oh, she's the one," and I'm like, "How do you know? You're not dating her." So I tend not to bring people home anymore.

Geof Barkley—My mom says that she can still baby me because when I come home, I'm all hers. When my brothers come home, they split time between our family and their in-laws. I don't have to do any of that stuff, and my mom kind of likes that. She cooks for me. She does my laundry when I'm there. So in that way it is different. She tries her best to make me feel like a kid again, tries to take care of me. My mom is absolutely the greatest.

Pam Thum—I think people tend to think you're a little more stable when you're married. I don't know why that is. I think people always take me as a little girl who will grow up when I get married. And I see my parents going, "We can't wait till we have a little Pammy." I don't think the public thinks that.

Cherie Paliotta, Avalon—My father is one of those proud Italians. He has a hard time letting me go. So, the longer I wait to get married is fine with him. He's really in no hurry.

Rebecca St. James, 40 Days with God—*One of the things that's really helped our family life is our "no secrets" policy. We have a commitment to do things together. When we were going through our "living by faith" experience, Mum and Dad would tell us about every desperate financial and physical need and share with us exactly what was going on. When God provided for our needs, we knew how incredible those miracles were. Even when we lived in Australia and Dad was promoting concerts, we would all go, even staying at the auditorium until two in the morning, just to be together.*

Now we home-school and travel as much as we can as a family. That has allowed us to become friends. We can talk about everything and especially spiritual matters. Our family is a team.²

Grover Levy—*My family knows that if I were expected to bring a covered dish, it wouldn't happen. I'm the guy who brings the two-liter Mountain Dew, that kind of thing.*

Dennis Rainey, Family Life Today—*For a number of years, I taught a graduate-level course to anywhere from three hundred to five hundred singles. The number one message (other than dating) that had the most hurt and the most need for clear biblical teaching was in the area of the fifth commandment, which commands us to honor our parents. There is a ton of unresolved bitterness, anger, and resentment. And as a result, we've got a whole generation of single people who are stymied in their Christian growth because they haven't dealt with what they're feeling toward their parents.*

Because single people don't have a spouse to force them to deal with issues related to their family of origin, there's a lot of business that has not been tended to in the single's life.

When a Friend Gets Married
"Will it ever happen for me?"

Lana—It just happened one week at my Bible study. A close friend got engaged. I wanted to be excited for her. I tried to ask questions and be interested in where the reception was going to be, what type of wedding dress she would wear, and where she would go on the honeymoon. However, deep inside, I was jealous. I wanted to be the one. I wanted to be there for her, but inside I wondered, *Will it ever happen for me?* The Bible says to rejoice with those who rejoice and mourn with those who mourn. In some instances, when a close friend of mine has gotten married, I have rejoiced for her but have mourned for the loss of her friendship. This time, I selfishly asked God, "Why not me?"

Dana—So, they've departed the world of singleness, exchanged vows before God, and entered the world of couplehood. It's not like they've left the planet. Or their new embarkment has hindered my receiving one of the three basic necessities—food, clothing, and shelter. So why does it suddenly feel like I've been deserted, left to go on in my world?

I could feel sorry for myself. I could get caught up in the idea that my best friend traded the late-night ice cream runs for male companionship and the random road trips with the gals for well-planned family vacations. But I don't want to mope around. I want to be okay that I'm not the one getting married. I want to be strong about realizing that I may not see my married friends as often. I don't really mind change; I just need a little time. When friends marry, I need to express my happiness for them, pray for their marriage, and quit focusing on myself.

Nathan—It was either very mystical or very contrived, but it happened over and over while I was still becoming and becoming—this degree, these expectations, this impossible schedule, projects, the fact that I nearly broke down and dropped out. I had to be someone first; I had to unbury myself. But all around me was this contriving, this pairing-up, this . . . Noah's arking. How did they do it? Two-by-two, they must have met suddenly and discussed the pluses and minuses, their fears, the need for a pastor to have a piano-playing wife, the fact that she came to college for the marrying more than the becoming or the learning.

> WHEN A FRIEND MARRIES, I TAKE IT AS AN OPPORTUNITY TO MEET A FEW BRIDESMAIDS. . . .
> —INTERNET CHAT ROOM COMMENT

And the pressure: "College is the best place to meet your mate. Once the demands of the world start, there will only be divorcees to choose from. You really should be thinking about what you're doing, the difficulties you are setting up for yourself. You should just take care of it."

The expenses of all my friends' weddings were mounting: tuxedo rentals; the obligations mounted: ushering. There were so many weddings right after college. Honestly, I couldn't understand how it all worked; how you met someone or suddenly dated someone who had been a classmate all along, and then willed to love to the extent that in a matter of months the two should become one.

I was concentrated, angst-ridden, a writer, a painter—or was trying to be those things. I had time only for ideas and paint. My friends were similar—writers and musicians. We sat on ice-cold steps outside of our dorm to ponder, we bought clothes from thrift stores, we were concerned with alternative sounds and haircuts. Domesticity was way out there and definitely a barrier to achievement. I hadn't the time. I hadn't the know-how. I couldn't marry. I had somehow missed that class, and I didn't possess the skills in romance and affection, neither wooing nor falling.

I was relegated to solitude.

Loneliness prowled out there. The people I needed, the ones I invested in, were pairing. I know I clung to them; I know I hung around when they needed me to get lost; I know I needed them too much when they had to concentrate on falling in love.

There was Lance. He was the best friend I had. He was my studio mate for two years, my roommate my last year—an artist with the unparalleled ability to be objective, rational, and structured. He could define his goals and then knock them down one by one. He had stated that he knew beyond a doubt that he wouldn't marry until five years after graduation when he was living in a city and had gained an art director's job. He knew where he was going.

And, without his input, my ideas never popped from their buds. We catalyzed each other's work. We brewed ideas for paintings, graphics studies, contemporary Plexiglas things, names for airbrush works like Mesopotamia, Vespers, and Variation I. We sketched on the walls; we sometimes had to wear masks to prevent dying from chemical smells. We were an innovative team, and people loved to hang out in our studio.

Eventually Kathy hung out there, too, and eventually she got Lance.

After only a month of their dating, Lance told me in our studio that he and Kathy were discussing marriage. Now I would be alone. Now I would have to go to New York totally alone.

After graduating, I took a trip to New York to feel it out. They had to save for their wedding. I bought a business that obligated me to stay in my small hometown. They moved away.

I would date and become excited about prospects, pull my married friends into it, want them to be happy for me, want their blessing, only to have the dating relationships fall apart. I always felt foolish; I always felt like the nonadult. I could not let go of the investment I had put into my former studio mate. I could not heal the gnawed edges I had suffered from being, in some part, replaced. I could not face the fear I had of the arduous process of finding my own soul mate, not even knowing if she was out there.

Over the years, inevitability arrives at your doorstep and grace through the growth of time helps you accept it. Lance and I see each other only every three to six months. You know how college friendships turn out even though you swear they never will. We talk frequently on the phone and through e-mail, and Kathy is as good a friend as Lance ever was. We are invested in each other's lives, and my friendships have doubled. They want me on their vacations. But careers rule our schedules.

Now, looking back, I know I needed to have the people I clung to move away from me so I could learn to cling to God. I do better now, but I still turn the other way sometimes and do stupid things. I know repentance and time on my knees in prayer that I didn't before. I have my space to work on my baggage, and, piece by piece, as it's revealed to me, I turn it over to God.

God has taught me that doubt is really sin and disbelief. He brings people through my life and challenges me to love them without any promise that they will stay or love me back. He lets me know that I may some day be blessed with a mate—no promises. It is not a thing that I must go get, that I need to work out, or that I need to have in order to become whole. If I will ever have this other person, it will only be after I have been prepared and torn down before God.

I am whole because I am God's. My search is for Him, my meaning is worked out daily in trying to be like Christ. I fall down all the time and display a lousy example of His love, but I pray that each time I fall, I don't go as far and people will eventually be pointed to Him.

I now see that I wasn't prepared eight or nine years ago for a mate and may not be for a while yet. I am, not because of my marital state. I am, not because of my artistic desires or because of any other label. I can be committed to these things, yes, but I am because I am God's.

In the process of living I am learning to understand that loneliness can't happen if I fill myself with God. Yes, the feelings can fly through, but I ignore them and accept being alone with God.

Chris—You knew it was coming. You saw her less and less each month for the last year. They looked good together, and he *is* a great guy. Her eyes would glisten when she spoke of him, and she'd giggle a little more with him around.

She calls and says that she has some important news and that she'll be right over. You already know what comes next: the wedding plans are all she can talk about for the next six months when you manage to get together, and then she's gone.

We get tense and a little anxious when one in our circle is getting married. Maybe it's some jealousy, but if it is, it is going two ways: we're jealous of our friend who now will "live happily ever after," and we're jealous of the spouse-to-be because we just lost a friend, either partly or entirely. We can feel the change in motion and that's upsetting.

Susan leaned against the door frame at the party. Others were having a good time, but I made the mistake of asking how she was. She proceeded to tell me that everyone had left her. She had belonged to a small group, and, over the years, each one left to get married. They rarely call. She grumbled on about how it will never be the same and that I, at my young age, couldn't understand. Susan, who looked just over thirty, was consumed with bitterness.

I got a taste of what Susan felt when a friend from my Bible study group announced one day that she had been dating someone pretty seriously for a while. That alone floored me. I thought we were friends. But I guess sometimes those dating know that if they share too much it may not seem real, or they'll jinx it, or the single they are sharing with won't understand or will be jealous or something. What seemed like three weeks later, she came to the study with a ring on her finger and waited for someone to notice, which was when she reached for a roll at dinner. Then she squealed with excitement and told us how he asked while we tried to smile and ask questions. But the whole time we were asking ourselves, *How could this go so quickly?* She dropped our group soon after because wedding plans consumed her. Besides seeing her for one day before the wedding, where she asked if I'd be willing to help serve cake at the reception and the actual wedding day, I've not seen her.

I guess I thought we had a friendship, but she cut me off. It seemed that she had limited time for friends, and she had a few closer ones than me.

In our singles' group, we will unofficially say that someone has "graduated" when they get married. This term is frowned upon because we are only restating what our self-esteems have been battling: that we aren't whole or grown-up or complete yet.

Other Voices

Cherie Paliotta, Avalon—*[When friends marry], I think their priorities change, which they should. In some cases, there is friendship neglect, and that is not good, but if I am a true friend, I have to understand that family needs to come first. So* as a single, that is something you have to expect. When your friends get married, their spouses and their children have to come before you and your friendship with that person. You realize you have to take a backseat.

Rich Mullins—The cool thing was that by the time Beaker got married, I was able really to rejoice with him. It was one of those cool things. Jesus talks about how the friend of the groom rejoices. Beaker's fiancée and I were friends as well. I really liked her. And I could see when they were courting, she really helped something develop in Beaker that I never could have and something that most likely wouldn't have developed outside of her. But the coolest thing was that I just saw two people who were really in love. And even if you're not going to participate in that, when you see it happening, you say, "Wow, that's great."

I think when I was younger it was hard when my friends got married, because I was gonna have to find someone else to hang out with. And they're gonna be home making passionate love, and I was gonna be home watching television. But I think as you get older you realize that married people don't very frequently make passionate love, and single people do a lot more than watch television. So you begin to see why it's not all it's cracked up to be. They are both really much more.

I'll Never Do That at My Wedding
"All you single girls come down to catch the bouquet."

Chris—I'll never make my good friends dress in pink, frilly gowns meant for an eighties junior high formal. Well, maybe to get back at them for the ever-growing "never-wear-again" section of my closet.

Single and Content

I'll never throw the bouquet. This is a stupid tradition where all the single girls are supposed to run up on the dance floor and giggle as they push their way to the promise of being the next to marry. Lately, at the weddings I've attended, only those under twenty-five seem so giddy as those of us who are a bit older try to hide in the shadows.

I'll never call on my single friends, by name over the microphone, to quit hiding and come down for the bouquet toss. This happened to me twice this year. It didn't work either. I just looked around, as did everyone else, for those the bride named.

Lana—Have you ever gone to a wedding and had a woman usher? I was one once and definitely won't ever have one. I was glad to be a part of the bridal party, but it was awkward. A male usher will take a woman's arm when he seats a group. I didn't know what to do. Was I supposed to take the man's arm? I ended up walking and then pointing. I also hated facing the crowd and releasing the different rows. I kept thinking, *Am I unzipped?*

The age of video is definitely here, and its role in weddings is changing. One couple wanted to make sure they saw everyone who came to their reception. They placed a video camera at the buffet line. It made me uncomfortable. I felt I needed to block my food from the camera in case they were going to send a bill.

Dana—It seems like I am always going to or participating in someone else's wedding. This year I'm involved in nine weddings from June through October. I feel like I have temporarily surrendered my life to become a professional wedding participant.

Actually, I like weddings, but at many of them, I can't get

past those silly traditions such as the garter or bouquet toss—that singles' cattle call that can draw unwanted attention to all the unmarried ones attending. But even worse than that is the trauma caused from realizing—invitation in hand—that I have less than three weeks to find a date to the wedding. After showing up dateless time after time, I'd much rather have that friend, acquaintance, or just an attractive "arm piece" to accompany me there, instead of hoping to strike up comfortable conversation with those sitting near me.

I can remember last year suffering through that very trauma as I contemplated asking my friend Jonathan to an upcoming wedding. I loved being around him and knew that we would have a great time, but I didn't want to give him the wrong—or right—idea. How could I ask him in a way that was nonthreatening to our friendship? How could I ask him in a casual, not premeditated way, yet make it obvious to him that I really wanted his company over someone else's?

Sounds kind of like high school, doesn't it? Fortunately, the asking and accepting went smoothly. It was fairly painless. I think we even had a good time.

Nathan—They kissed. They were introduced to the congregation as Mr. and Mrs. So-and-So. They strode triumphantly out of the sanctuary to Mendelssohn followed by their entourage. It was complete. Then, they scurried back in to the front of the church. I felt my face go hot with mortification for them. They must have forgotten something. The ring? No. They did that. The communion? Taken care of. Was it some little phrase they had forgotten to repeat back to the minister? Were they not legal yet? Nope. They were going to greet their guests, and they promptly started hugging and kissing people at the front of the church and proceeded to the back. It was like when the play is over and all the actors come out on stage to take a bow and jolt the audience back to reality. I found it ridiculous. Still do. I know a bride and groom are obligated to greet all their guests and don't want to miss anyone. But instead of this show, they should get their guests fed and make the rounds to the individual tables themselves.

I hope to avoid the whole garter thing too. Aren't we supposed to be Christians? Doesn't that mean we should at least show a modicum of decency at a wedding reception? After an entire afternoon of proper etiquette, everyone seems intent on sleazing it up at the end as the groom practically undresses the woman he is supposed to love, in front of her parents and the whole room of guests, and then flings part of her underthings out to his bachelor buddies. That won't happen at my shindig.

Holiday Hoopla Can Hurt
"This was supposed to be the year, and it wasn't."

Nathan—One evening, I was walking to my car from the mall. This was when I lived in a small town, so I wasn't surprised that I ran into a couple of my married friends. I was very glad to see them; I hadn't seen them in several weeks. It was chilly, so I hopped into their car to chat. They asked if I had eaten yet. I hadn't, so they invited me along.

Once at the restaurant and well through the meal, I realized that the restaurant was filled primarily with couples—no families or groups of people. Then I was embarrassed. They were so kind to invite me, but I should have graciously declined their offer and allowed them to dine alone on Valentine's Day.

The holiday had meant so little to me through the years. Not having been coupled with anyone on that date, I had forgotten it was even a holiday.

I can't remember the holidays ever being too hard on me. I

never have thought of them as a married person's day—believing they would be more enjoyable or fulfilling if only I were married. Thanksgiving and Christmas have always been a big family time when I can finally stop all the rushing and not feel guilty about going home, eating too much, and lying around the house with the rest of my family.

Our holidays are interesting because we generally have more than the family group there. Many years ago, a family that left communist Yugoslavia joined us for Christmas and soon was adopted into our family—mom, dad, and kid are now a part of all our family functions. Since the mother is an artist and the father and son are economics professors, our conversation ranges from art to culture to politics and is never dull. We occasionally have a Christian Pakistani family over also that my mom met at the mall.

My first year at our singles' ministry, I decided to go to the New Year's Eve banquet. They have a great formal dinner/dance for Christians who don't want to hang out with the boozer crowd. You don't have to have a date either, but you can hang out with your friends. I, however, had no friends yet in the group but decided to be very brave and independent. I went and ended up sitting at a sort of bachelors' table where I got investment tips for buying and fixing up rental properties. It was a fun time, but I didn't see those people again. I made my friends instead through working on the singles' newsletter for the group.

Lana—The holidays are ruled by the married people in our family. When it comes to planning when and where we meet, I'm not really consulted. It's assumed I can come any time. I call it the Cindy Brady syndrome. Actually, I understand they have two sets of families to try to squeeze in. It just seems sometimes that they don't realize that I have a life too.

Christmas is the hardest holiday for me. It lasts so long. From Halloween to December 26, our society is focused on Christmas. Our family is changing traditions. Most of my siblings have children and want Santa to visit at their house. So instead of having our double-elimination cribbage tournament on Christmas Eve and opening presents Christmas morning, we get together the week before or after. That leaves Christmas Eve open. Yuck.

The best Christmas Eve without the family was a couple of years ago. My roommate and I went to our Christmas Eve service and invited all the singles that we saw to come to our place. We were up till 3:00 in the morning playing cards, playing games, and watching *The Princess Bride.* It has become a tradition. Some years are better than others. Last year, it was just two guys and me. But it was two guys and me! Not bad odds.

The office Christmas party can be an extremely threatening event. Luckily, a friend helped me out and came to my last office's Christmas party. He's a great conversationalist and people like him. He's not a romantic interest, but I had a good time and didn't feel so singled out.

Our singles' ministry really helps to make New Year's Eve bearable. We have our own dinner/dance. I might not have anyone to kiss when the clock hits midnight, but there are plenty of friends to hug. And it just seems fitting to have an event to dress up for.

Valentine's Day can be a bummer if I'm not dating someone. One year, we had a President's Day party instead. We just ignored the hearts, the candy, and the cupids and focused on our American presidents.

Dana—My cousin was in her senior year of college when she came and joined the family at my parents' house for Thanksgiving. She arrived in her college sweats, as cheery as always— but this time something was different. She had brought someone along: her fiancé. Wow! I was happy for them both but was made completely aware of who was soon to be married and who wasn't. Actually I knew beforehand of her engagement, but the reality of it all descended at Thanksgiving. I was not bitter, just a little amazed at the timing of our lives. Here I was, well out of college and definitely into the single, independent woman category, and my little cousin, who used to talk school camp stories for hours, was preparing to tie the knot. It was a bit overwhelming. After all the praying and knowing how to find contentment in the Lord, regardless of the situation, I couldn't shake that "Is it ever going to be me?" feeling.

But then there's that day of red hearts, where talk is mushy and nearly all restaurants have at least a ninety-minute wait. The last two Valentine's Days, I showed up to work in black. That was my way of celebrating the holiday while wives and girlfriends received roses and chocolates. I tried to make a joke of it, like I was in mourning or something. It actually worked for me, kept things light. I even bought a half-dozen chocolate chip cookies one year from a coworker's wife. She had made each cookie on a long white stick wrapped in red, heart-shaped foil and placed all of them in a long, slender white box, like roses. I took the "roses" and delivered them around town to my friends. I loved surprising them.

Chris—Holidays are holidays to me. They aren't particularly hard. I've not had the tragic breakup just days before New Year's Eve or ever struggled with what to buy a guy for Christmas. I've not had good relationship experiences around the holidays, nor have I had bad experiences. So to me holidays are holidays. They usually consist of me going home to see my family, which is fine. Only two of Mom and Dad's six kids are married, so we still are at the stage of welcoming new members around the Christmas tree.

One year my women's Bible study group got tired of spending Valentine's Day alone, so we planned a party. The ten of us made a home-cooked meal for the ten guys we invited, and their job was to bring a Valentine's gift for us. We randomly matched up couples and played a few games like "The Newly Met Game." It was a relaxed, fun environment, and even though it wasn't meant to be a matchmaking event, one of the couples we matched up got married a year and a half later.

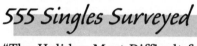

555 Singles Surveyed

"The Holiday Most Difficult for Me Is…"

Under the age of 30
1. Valentine's Day
2. Christmas
3. New Year's Eve
4. Thanksgiving

Over the age of 30
1. Christmas
2. Valentine's Day
3. New Year's Eve
4. Thanksgiving

Other Voices

Heather Floyd, Point of Grace—I've never had a good Valentine's Day, except last year when I went on a singles' retreat in Houston for the weekend. We had a seventies prom. Everybody dressed up in horrible dresses with horrible hair and horrible shoes and they were playing all this seventies music. It was a blast. It was a lot of fun. So I have had one good Valentine's Day.

Michael Passons, Avalon—I blow off Valentine's Day. I have *enough single friends that we'll all get together and have this big anti–Valentine's Day party and make each other feel better. Christmas is more difficult, probably because of past Christmases when I have had someone to share it with. And every single Christmas song that isn't about God is about spending it with your "baby." So it is drilled into your head that Christmas is a time to be intimate. My parents may give me a little bit more at Christmas time. Not having a spouse, you have more gift-giving time. My mom may say, "Here's just one more present, but don't tell anybody."*

Max Hsu, Church of Rhythm—*I was alone at sixteen in the U.S., so I learned to manage holidays without a family. I kind of turned that part of me off. A couple of Christmases I got a lot of work done, because no one called me. Holidays don't really faze me. I care a lot more than I used to because the girls I've dated did.*

Pam Thum—*Christmas is always a lonely time. I don't really know why; I have everyone around me and it's wonderful. But I think a long time ago, when I was a teenager, my first boyfriend and I broke up or something because ever since, I have felt a little down. . . . I love Christmas and New Year's. I love them. I'm like a little kid on New Year's especially, because I think it's another year and I think of all that I haven't done and all I need to do and it takes about a month for me to get over the pressure of what I should have accomplished by that time in my life.*

Nikki Hassman—*My family dotes on me at Christmas time since I was engaged when I was nineteen. They are worried that it is hard for me since I am not with that special guy. They say things like, "Maybe next year . . ."*

Janna Potter, Avalon—New Year's is a tough holiday. I love my girlfriends dearly, but I don't want to kiss them when the clock strikes midnight.

Going to Reunions
"You haven't changed a bit. . . . Are you married?"

Chris—I just went to my ten-year high school reunion last July. It was weird. Everybody looked old.

I was home by 10:00 because I was so bored. All you do is walk around and try to summarize ten years in three sentences or less. And within that paragraph, you have to share your marital status with optional inclusion of the kids' pictures, your current job status, and then some cute or funny story. Well, if I wasn't interested in their lives in the last decade, why would I want an update now? I was curious, though, about what course they took in their lives.

Within the first ten minutes, I made eye contact with an old boyfriend. Since most others had their wives or husbands with them, he asked if he could sit with me, and we sat down as old movie flashbacks of re-sparking romances surfaced. We were able to talk beyond the three-sentence quota, and, even after separating to mingle, we came back together when we noticed that both of us were laughing at the idiots on the dance floor who still remembered how to dance to the eighties hits. He finally looked at me seriously and said that he needed to tell me something. He very confidently told me that he was gay and that he'd moved to Arizona. He's quite happy, and he just wanted someone in the room to know.

I tried to remain calm and understanding. I made a joke, asking him if I had anything to do with it, but I was quite uneasy. So I could continue a conversation with my gay ex-boyfriend, or I could break dance with the thirty-year-olds, or I could try to blend in to the clique over by the bar.

I opted for the latter route. After sharing my three sentences, I listened to those around me.

Even though I joke about my reunion, I realized there that I don't live in the real world. Most of the people I hang out with now are college-educated Christians, but most of my graduating class didn't pursue higher education, and they continue to live with a high school mentality. Many continue to live in the high school morality too.

I didn't feel bad being one of the few never-marrieds in the room; I was different in so many ways—being a college-educated Christian who moved more than ten miles from home—so one more thing didn't matter.

It's kind of like when Mom used to tell me in elementary school: "Someone can't pick on you unless you let them." They can't bother you unless you are already bothered by what truth they choose to twist or look down on. I am not bothered by my singleness, and I definitely wouldn't switch lives with most of them, so my thoughts were better occupied wondering if I could still moonwalk.

Dana—I graduated in a class of 142 in the rural community of Salem, Indiana. Our class had no five-year reunion, so we opted for a seven-year instead. It was held at an adorable little house out in the country. I made the drive across the winding gravel roads amid the grassy fields and cattle fences to find a yard full of 1988 classmates sitting back, enjoying the sunny afternoon. I have to admit it was a bit awkward as I approached the crowd, feeling somewhat out of place wearing my summer dress, as cutoffs, T-shirts, and tennis shoes would've been more appropriate. I hadn't seen most of the people there since graduation day, but regardless of their altered appearance, I was quick to recognize them. The cluster of conversing graduates made me snicker inside. It seemed the gals that I might consider a bit abrasive or rougher than most were hanging around with the scholastic, athletic types. These gals were talking about their kids, some with three or four. There were no walls, no barriers. Time had erased the cliques, and everyone was at ease sharing their stories.

Then there was me.

I gravitated to the ones I knew well and observed the ones I never hung out with. Though I had expected that most would be married, engaged, or living together, I still felt in the minority because I wasn't even dating anyone. It didn't seem appropriate to bring up most of what my life is about. I wanted to say, "Let me tell you about my home in Indianapolis and the wonderful singles' ministry I am involved with." But it didn't seem to fit with the tattoo inquiries, the latest local bar stories, and

> ### How to Be Successful without Really Trying
>
> Wear a fake wedding band and repeatedly say how sorry you are that your spouse couldn't make it because he/she would love to meet your old friends. Unfortunately, he/she is (*a*) closing a deal on a private Caribbean island, (*b*) on a top-secret initiative in the Middle East, or (*c*) running a halfway house for former child stars and there was trouble on the "Different Strokes" wing.
>
> Taken from Michael Nolan and Eve Sarrett, *I'm So Tired of Other People, I'm Dating Myself* (Nashville, Tenn: Thomas Nelson Publishers, 1993).

the popular desire to fix up old houses in Salem and settle down. But that was okay. I enjoyed the day for its main purpose: to see, hear, and catch up. I actually had a refreshing conversation with the class valedictorian. She, too, was unmarried, and she was about to leave for a year-long mission trip in Holland. Finally, I could actually relate.

Lana—My friends from college get together every year at the Schaeffers' farm in Mentone, Indiana. It's neat to see my friends' children growing up, and I'm so thankful that we keep in touch. Some years I have a great time there, and, sometimes, I spend the entire time secretly focused on my singleness and how I want to be married and have kids. My friends treat me the same each year; I'm the only one focused on being different.

I think I'm learning how to handle these reunions the best way. One tactic is to resort to trying to be the super-single: "Did I tell you about my three-week trip to Australia or how my job is going so well?" As if to make them think, *Don't I wish I were single again?* But the real challenge is when everyone is sharing pictures and I can only say, "Do you want to see my most recent driver's license photo?" The better strategy is to recognize when I'm not feeling secure in my singleness and, when a family discussion comes up, move to another one.

The last time we got together a friend was discussing how she's concerned with her third pregnancy. She's concerned because she's not so young anymore. Her feelings and concerns are valid, and it was totally appropriate for her to share this. However, I was thinking, *Well, gosh, I haven't had any kids yet, and I'm older than you.* So instead of sitting there and getting upset, I asked another single friend to go for a walk and chat. However, as time marches on, finding a single friend to chat with gets harder and harder.

Nathan—My ten-year high school reunion was four years ago. Given that, I still don't worry much about aging. My motto when I turned thirty was "My thirties are going to be phenomenal."

I went to the reunion only because my best friend was going to be there, and he told me I had to go so he would have someone to talk to. The thought of still being single didn't even cross my mind. I was more nervous about having to see the people who snubbed me all through school. Being single at this time hadn't weighed on me, as I viewed myself as just starting out and not needing any encumbrances. I went in and chatted with many people I would have barely spoken to in high school. No one asked about my marital status, as they probably never expected me to marry in the first place, having been a nerd in many of their eyes. People seemed genuinely interested in where I was living, what I was doing, and if I had, in fact, become an artist.

The only time the single thing flickered through my brain was when they handed out those goofball awards. One girl got the award for having been married the longest—ten years. Then I thought, *She's got a whole decade on me.* But that was about it.

Other Voices

Mark Wesner, Singles Minister—The guys in high school who were smoking, drinking, and fighting out in the parking lot were the ones who, twenty years later, were still smoking, drinking, and fighting out in the parking lot! Some things never change, or grow up, for that matter.

Feeling Puny and Wanting Mommy
"I don't feel so good."

Chris—There is nothing worse than having to shop for yourself when you're sick. Last September, I came down with what people would call the common cold, but it is never common to the one who is sick. I stared at the endless aisles of medicines, drops, pills, and syrups. I was overwhelmed. Which goes with which? Which can I mix to make myself better but not cause brain damage?

I walked over to the pharmacist with four bottles in my hands.

Through a scratchy, almost nonexistent voice, I mumbled, "Help."

When I'm sick, I want everyone to know it. I lie on the couch in the middle of the house, loaded down with Mom's quilt, Kleenex, and cough drops.

I moan a lot. I want everyone to have a constant reminder: "Hey, she's sick over there." If my voice is scratchy, it's even better. I feel rewarded when I get a "poor baby" or get sympathetic looks.

Nathan—I think a big upside to having a roommate would be the help you'd get during episodes of illness, assuming he'd care to be around when you've got your face in the toilet or you have been moaning loudly. A roommate who truly loves you would stick around for that. It's good to have someone go out for you to buy Sprite and then put bendy straws in it.

Not only does it stink to be sick, but it double stinks to be alone and sick. Then, take me: it stinks to be sick and alone, but I hate someone doting over me. So I require that extra special balance of someone around who puts bendy straws in my Sprite and makes sure that I don't need to be rushed to the emergency room but who stays out of the way and doesn't try to make me eat Jell-O or shower after three days.

One weekend in July, I took my girlfriend, a nurse practitioner, to Michigan to get acquainted with my friends. On Sunday afternoon during a board game I announced I was getting a cold. She and everybody at the table laughed their heads off because I was so resolute about it. I am. I know the exact moment that I am getting a cold. It's when that tickle starts running down my throat and I start swallowing until my mouth is parched. They didn't believe me. She didn't believe me. She just told me to drink some orange juice and cupped her hand over her mouth to hide the fact that she was laughing at me. I spent the next three weeks (which is exactly how long my colds always linger) with the most horrendous virus, giving her updates over the phone. Don't think that you will get extra sympathy dating or marrying a medical professional; you will get sound medical advice ("Drink plenty of fluids") and the assurance that you will be okay once this is over. They see too much suffering at work and aren't in the mood for it at home. Who can blame them?

The worst time I got sick at work was when I came down with chills and body aches and I knew I was in for a doozy. At the time I functioned in a role that no one else could do, so the attitude was "finish this last lifesaving measure on this project and tie up a few loose ends before you hurl and go home." When I finally got into my car for the drive home, I was shaking. Then, I had to drive in freeway traffic and drag myself into my apartment only to realize I didn't have any flu remedies (Sprite or Jell-O). I think I decided to die instead of going to the grocery store to obtain the wonder drugs, and I burrowed under three blankets to shake for the rest of the evening.

I bet that married people visit the doctor a lot more. It seems like these folks are a lot more routine-oriented, and I can just envision wives making appointments for their husbands routinely and then notifying the men that they need to be at the doctor this week. I rarely go. No one makes me. In fact, my doctor is in another town since I never switched. I only go when I am sick, and that is usually something I will get over anyway, like a cold.

Dana—It's never fun being sick, and, even in my adult years, I still feel myself longing for my mom to come sit with me and hold that cool washcloth on my forehead. Isn't it amazing the things you remember from when you were a kid? I don't want to drive to the drug store for prescriptions when I'm queasy and off-balance. I'd give anything for that to be taken care of.

Independence suddenly looses a bit of appeal at these times. But thank goodness for friends. If you can't go to them, they can come to you. My friend once saved the day with a liter of ginger ale and ibuprofen. A little personal attention and concern will often provide a measure of comfort.

Sometimes, though, I'd rather not make contact with the outside world when I am sick. I don't feel like the same person, and, often, I don't even recognize the sickly person I see in my mirror. I remember being home from work for two consecutive days once with an ear infection. Anyone who has ever endured this nagging pain knows that it's not fun. There was no chance of a bit of relaxation while I tried to nurse myself back to health. But I had to laugh about the effect of the infection on my equilibrium! I already struggle with the balance thing every now and then, so any attempt at walking a straight line while enduring the ear infection was a failure. I remember hearing a knock on my door in the middle of the day, right when I was feeling the worst. Since I was already on my feet trying to convince myself that everything was going to be fine, I proceeded to the door. It was a sight that only I could truly appreciate and be amused by. I felt like a pinball, spinning toward one wall, bouncing across the hallway to the other wall, briefly making contact and persistently continuing forward, not really knowing what object I would come in contact with next. Eventually, I arrived at the door to find two nicely dressed, polite young gentlemen who wanted to talk with me for a while and share some information. Little did they know the little trauma I had endured just to answer the door. But I then had to somehow regain composure (while struggling to hear what they were saying) and explain why it might not be the best time for conversation.

Lana—The problem about being sick or injured and being single is the question, How much can I ask my roommates or friends to do? How much is taking advantage of them? I remember being in a car wreck and having to call a coworker to take me to the emergency room. I'm not sure what the line is between friend and coworker, but seeing me in that hospital gown had to be close to the line.

The other problem with being sick is that I never have food in the fridge. I remember getting the stomach flu on my first day at a new job. I woke up, and my stomach was acting funny. I diagnosed it as just nerves. Soon I was running into the women's bathroom, and no stall was available. The sinks were occupied as well. I really couldn't say, "Excuse me. I'm vomiting. Would you please make way?" I ended up trying to throw up in the indented trash can that was built into the wall. It wasn't very effective. I went home and cried. Here it was my first day on a new job, and I'd thrown up on myself. To make things worse, I had no food. No Jell-O. No 7-Up. No saltine crackers. Luckily, my parents lived about an hour away. My mom brought me food and took my vomit dress away.

Other Voices

Heather Floyd, Point of Grace—*I don't get sick very often, but when I do, I'm a big baby. You immediately want Mom because she was always there for you. Especially when I would throw up. She'd be there in the bathroom with me with a cold rag.*

Well we were somewhere in Illinois, and I had eaten this apple and marshmallow fruit salad. I wasn't very hungry, but I ate some of that. I started feeling so sick. We were fixing to do a concert, and I was in the bathroom throwing up. Michele was in there brushing her teeth and said, "Hey, are you throwing up?" And I was like, "Uh-uh. I don't feel good." I threw up before the concert. I threw up at intermission. I threw up after the concert. There was nothing I could do. When I was on stage I was fine, but immediately when I got off, I threw up. I just got on the bus and lay down. I rarely get sick, and that is probably why I'm such a baby when I do.

Rebecca St. James, 40 Days with God—*I remember one time last year when I [had] three concerts in twenty-seven hours. The worst part was that I was the sickest that I'd been in a long time. I really had no voice, so I prayed that God would heal me. I walked out on stage and asked people to pray for me and ask God to work through the situation for all of us. I didn't get healed immediately, but my voice got progressively stronger as I sang. I felt broken, like I had nothing to give at all. Yet, this experience taught me when we are weakest, God is strong.*[3]

4

Looking for the Holy Grail Woman—or Man
(Dating)

In the local bookstore, the "Singles" section overwhelmingly contains books on how not to be single. We are told how to find the love of our lives or how to prepare to be the best marriage partner. Our book, by design, is not intended as a dating guide or a meet-your-mate handbook. However, the subject cannot be skipped. We are defined as single because we are not part of a double. The process of becoming a couple is often on our minds, especially since the majority of secular music, TV, and movies is focused on the topic. This chapter covers the good, the bad, the ugly, and the humorous parts of dating. We hope it will encourage you, as you probably can relate.

The Media's Impact on Dating
"They've really sold us a lie."

Lana—Today it seems that it's more socially acceptable to have been married and then divorced than never to have been married. At least someone wanted them once. Never-marrieds naturally wonder, "Why doesn't anyone want me?" I need to remind myself that this question would only make sense if there were no God who cares for me. It's not that no one wants me—it's that right now, God wants me single. I might not understand His timetable, but I know He loves me. I have to work to have faith in that.

Also, society views us as incomplete without a spouse. The famous line in the movie *Jerry McGuire*—"You complete me"—communicates that if you're not married, then you are incomplete. This view even permeates some Christian circles. An ad for a Christian matchmaking service on the Internet says, "Find your other half." This statement isn't biblical. In marriage, God takes two whole individuals, not two halves, and makes them one. Jesus wasn't half a person. The apostle Paul and Mother Teresa weren't half-persons. If we have a personal relationship with Jesus, then we are complete in Christ.

My values and the principles in the Bible seem pretty strange compared to those reflected in the media. In college, when I watched my soap operas, I was amazed how I would want a couple to get together even though each was married to someone else. A more recent TV show made these opposing values really clear. In this episode, everyone puts down a guy because he's never had a one-night stand. This floored me. I thought society's take on sex was that if you really love the person, then sex is okay. Here, they were criticizing a man because he never had meaningless sex. I feel like such an alien—as if I can be put in some type of zoo simply because I'm waiting to be sexually active.

Chris—Roommates and I find it a rare treat when all three of us are home on a Thursday evening to watch the Thursday night TV lineup, instead of watching the videotape on Saturday morning and shushing the people all day Friday who try to tell us the good parts.

No one on these popular shows is married, or at least not happily married. Contrary to all propaganda hitting us from all sides telling us that we *need* to have someone, these shows seem to understand us. And we understand them. *Friends* is for those in their late twenties, still seeking their spot in life. *Seinfeld* talks about nothingness, yet says so much to so many, especially those in their thirties.

The humor grabs me in these shows. The writing is so good. *ER,* besides having a healthy share of guys to look at, offers a story line that keeps us wanting more. We all sigh and pout when the credits fade in after a dramatic pause.

Everybody loves a love story. It gives us a romantic hope. But the problem with movies or TV plots is that they mostly revolve around the passion and intrigue of finding someone, and we see and feel the desire for a "happily ever after" relationship. Yet they still focus more on the physical rather than getting to know the person. The characters fall in love in two days and just know it is right. This makes for a great movie, but what happens a year later? Can we follow the lovers to see what love is like when life isn't so spontaneous?

At least 90 percent of the songs we hear on the radio center around relationships. America is in love with being in love. Rarely do we hear songs that capture the selflessness that God wants a husband and wife to have. Jesus taught us that true love is serving and thinking of the other person first.

555 Singles Surveyed

"I Watch Four Hours or Less of TV Each Week."

Men   49%
Women 63%

A.C. Neilson Company's national average is twenty-eight hours per week for the average adult.

Dana—As a Christian, I have to be especially careful not to be judgmental. I know I need to move outside my places of comfort and face this crass society and accept that life can be ugly and disappointing. I am so tired of hearing about people, even our nation's leader, with poor judgment and little attention to morals and values. Our society is becoming one that embraces sin in order to avoid conflict or adversity instead of standing up for what is right. If having any conscience at all is too much to ask, I guess abiding by Christian principles based on God's Word would really be asking for too much.

I used to watch TV a lot, but I wouldn't say I ever just sat in front of the television for hours, just because I had nothing better to do. It was nice to come home from a long day at work and meet up with my friends in that weekly emergency room drama or just tune in to some shows and laugh for a while. But now, even some of the "good" shows bother me. Yeah, the shows are funny, but most of the humor is based on meaningless sexual experiences with people they never hope to see again. Some recent shows feature lesbian lovers dealing with everyday life, trying to paint a picture of normalcy and acceptance.

But it seems controversy sells. We viewers fall into a trap, believing that some television content won't eventually get to us or influence us in negative ways. But it can. I have gotten to the point where a few laughs aren't so worth it anymore. I don't want to be tolerant of influences that can cause me to rationalize sin. Society and TV don't seem to encourage people to be pure, holy, and blameless before the Lord. They instead glorify convenient sex before marriage, lying and cheating, and pleasure-seeking motives focused on self and personal gain.

Everybody has a choice. I've got feelings and desires and hormones like everybody else, but I don't want to disappoint the Lord by acting on selfish desires. Sin separates us from the One who loves us the most, and I want to be right with Him. The

Lord is trying to protect me, not limit my life experiences. So why does our society have to blur the truth, minimizing the consequences of our actions and making it seem ridiculous to act in good conscience?

Nathan—I think that if something makes us more susceptible to sin, then we should stay away from it. We're all aware that the television and music industries' objectives are not to edify; they are to entertain. I've had to decide recently what I want entertainment to be for me. I am solely responsible for the attitude of my heart, and, if certain lyrics or images would cause me to dwell too long on the baser side of my nature, I've had to avoid them.

It really isn't surprising to me what has become entertainment these days. A world without God is always going to spiral downward. As Christians, I think we should expect this tendency more than anyone; because we know the truth we should know what is inevitable if the truth is ignored.

It's hard to be single while we are inundated with "modern" ideas of morality. Our vision somehow gets clouded, and things that we know are wrong start to seem okay and justifiable. I don't like to refer to these times as "modern"; the term "modern" has a connotation of somehow being evolved, changed, more progressive. And when we label our current day like this, we start to believe that we are somehow living in a society that is no longer "old-fashioned," that the progress of modern man has superseded the commands of God. But, there is no new sin. Premarital sex, "alternative" sexual preferences, lust, hate, envy, murder, and deceit have always been around in the exact forms they are practiced today. There's nothing new.

Even the level of acceptance of these unbiblical practices isn't new. "Progressive" attitudes are simply a callous justification for what we are doing wrong—an attitude that all anyone needs for justification of his actions is the status of "consenting adult" and the claim that he is not hurting anyone else. In fact, we feel that the right to sleep with whomever we want, whenever we want, is a freedom, a birthright, for being an American. What we refuse to own up to is that freedom comes with greater responsibility than slavery.

It's amazing to me the double standard that goes on. Kids are taught that no one should have sex until she or he is ready and that the best situation in which to practice sex is a loving relationship. You usually see it played out on a TV sitcom (so that the rest of America will know just how to handle this delicate issue). The loving parent tells the teenager that sex is best experienced when she is ready and with someone she truly loves. When the preteen asks how she will know when she is ready, she usually gets an answer like "You'll just know. . . ." Isn't it always the case that when the non-Christian world is pressed for an absolute answer they can only come up with a piece of relativistic fluff like this, which means absolutely nothing and remains open-ended for everyone's interpretation, not pinning down the dispenser of such grand "wisdom"?

The sexuality that is fragile in your childhood is also fragile in your adulthood, but that fact is ignored. If someone reaches adulthood, or even passes the age of eighteen, and is unmarried and still suffering from that woeful burden known as virginity, then people immediately assume something is wrong with him. So what's going on here? Is there a magic age at which, if you have not felt that you are "ready" and are not in a loving relationship, it is time to toss your virginity to the wind for the sake of experience and valid entrance into society? I think that this laissez-faire attitude is thrown around in order to cover up the suffering of those who do throw away their virginity before marriage. People who experience casual sex but can't seem to shake the guilt or feelings of betrayal must form a social club whose motto is "It's okay. Everyone is doing it."

Premarital sex is not okay and, no, not everyone is doing it. And those who are abstaining are actually carrying around considerably fewer suppressed feelings of anguish than those who are not abstaining outside of marriage.

If we begin to think that it is hard to stay pure when "everyone else is doing it," I think we should stop and make ourselves realize that sex is not for us single people. It was solely created with very specific reasons for those who have married. We should learn to ask for help from God when we first notice the onset of those feelings. God does not want us slipping into sin; don't you think He will lend help if we ask for strength and power to avoid it?

555 Singles Surveyed

"My Favorite TV Show Is..."
1. ER
2. Seinfeld
3. Friends
4. Sports
5. Touched by an Angel
6. Ally McBeal
7. The X-Files
8. News
9. Frasier
10. Party of Five

Other Voices

Gary Mullet—*We just get this constant barrage of immorality from the media. The most popular shows on TV, Friends and all this stuff, it's one sexual innuendo after another. Before you know it, this stuff just becomes so commonplace that there is a real danger of it creeping into your everyday life. And it makes it tough.*

Looking for the Holy Grail Woman—or Man

Cherie Paliotta, Avalon—It's all over the TV, magazines, videos, and the movies. Everywhere you look there are negative influences, and, as a Christian, you just have to take the stance that you are going to fight this thing.

Pam Thum—In general people are waiting to get married because there is a lot of fear. I watch TV. I click the channels and there are not very many good examples of happy marriages. To me, it's a circle that produces fear in people that affects the masses. If you fill your mind with the idea that everyone is going to go out on you—that's not the case. Not everybody goes out on everybody. There's so much fear that TV and the media put into you. People are scared to give a part of themselves and scared to trust.

Michael Passons, Avalon—People are very disillusioned. They don't really know what love is. [This distorted view is] filtered into our minds, and it starts at a very early age. We need to keep in mind the ideals God set for love and for marriage.

Rebecca St. James, 40 Days with God—The first time I heard the song "You're the Voice" was when I was just a little kid in Australia. It was such a powerful song that many my age still remember it from their childhood. To me, it is a total call to our generation to not be silent, to not compromise. We are God's mouthpiece, His voice, to share with people the truth—that life is about living for Him and not living for ourselves.

The secular media (music, television, etc.) has really sold us a lie that life is about just doing what "feels good." Unfortunately, this generation has listened to that voice and accepted it as truth. But there is only one truth. And He needs to be the voice that guides our lives.[1]

Michael Medved, Film Critic—There has been a shift. Television overwhelmingly used to portray married couples, but the sense that I would have is that, particularly among new shows, they more often than not portray single people, people who are divorced, single mothers, and people who are not in conventional marriages.

I don't think that it is as simple to say that people in the networks respond to the public want. They don't necessarily do that. They help to create demand. Again, what you're talking about, in the cases of creating those shows, like Jerry Seinfeld, who is single into his forties, is that people tend to write about or create what they know. Also, everyone who is married has been single and to some extent can relate to that or recall what that was like, where particularly today for a lot of single people being married is more difficult to imagine.

Above everything else, TV and movies about singles create very unrealistic romantic expectations. They do that in terms of the way they portray the ease, or the relative ease, of meeting people. And they also feature the great attractiveness of all singles. You don't see a lot of film and TV shows about single characters who are grossly overweight or whose faces are asymmetrical, and yet in real life there are lots and lots of people like that. What this creates, of course, is the idea that unless your dance card looks like the cast of Friends, you're somehow missing out on your inalienable sexual entitlement.

Dating and the Christian Perspective
"Aren't there any nice boys at church?"

Chris—When I mention to a married friend, especially to a non-Christian, that I attend a singles' group, I can see that they automatically assume the picture of depressed, desperate people hanging out around a punch bowl awkwardly trying to make conversation. When they find out how big the group is and how long I've been involved, they are puzzled that I still don't have someone. People are always asking me, "Aren't there any nice boys at church?"

I'm learning how rare it is to have a singles' ministry like ours that has a purpose of worshiping God and getting to know Him better. The three-hundred-member group serves in fifteen ministry areas, from small group Bible studies and service projects to evangelism and fellowship. Sure, we host lots of social activities, but serving God and having fun as a Christian are always the focus. Sure, we have lots of marriages and successful relationships, but most of us have developed great friendships that will last too. And sure, we are serious about our ministry, but we also enjoy being surrounded by people like us, who are single and trying to live the path God has laid out for us.

Beyond the singles' group, though, I haven't sought out other ways for meeting guys. I can't see myself walking into a dating service. It seems too aggressive to me.

After reading Joshua Harris's book *I Kissed Dating Goodbye*, I can honestly say that I agree with many of his points, but I'm not sure how practical they are. Even in the Christian circuit, dating seems appropriate. And my standards are so high already. I would like a chance at marriage.

Someone once said that if we want to know whom to date we should passionately run with what God has for us in ministry. Then, as we are running, we can look around at who is keeping up or running in the same direction.

Lana—I've always heard that "it" will happen when I least expect it. ("It" being falling in love, getting married, and having 2.3 children with the man of my dreams.) I'd like to believe that this is true and that I should just trust God and let it be. However, my "love, marriage, and kids" dream has a time limit attached to it. My biological clock is ticking. So, more than ever, I am open to different ways to meet men. I'm not desperate, but if I can help the process—great. The old expression "God helps those who help themselves" isn't in the Bible, but I think we can do things to help our chances.

A couple of years ago, one of the partners of my firm asked me out. He is attractive, quite a bit older, and not a Christian. The Bible says that we shouldn't be unequally yoked—Christians shouldn't date non-Christians. I also don't think it's advisable to date someone with whom you work. It can get really messy.

Lately, most of my dating experiences have occurred because I joined a Christian dating service or a friend fixed me up. I know some don't like blind dates, and they are stressful, but I think it's worth the risk. I've learned a lot and met some great guys. Also, the men who join dating services are interested in dating. When I meet men in other circles, I don't always know that. Right now, it's the same old routine. He'll like me or I'll like him, but rarely do we each like each other at the same time.

Probably the newest way for me to meet others is the Internet. I've met some online and a couple in person. Whoever does this must be extremely careful. I read about one Internet encounter in which a grad student tortured a girl for about thirty hours before she died. People can say anything on the Internet. When I finally met my online pal in Chicago, I brought a girlfriend along. We had a nice lunch. I was interested; he wasn't. Another Internet interest and I had nothing in common when we met, but it's hard to see all that in an e-mail. Right now, I'm going for more of the personal approach. But if I'm online and someone sends me an instant message, I'll chat. You never know.

Church is the best place to meet dating prospects, no contest. We should be drawn to others who share our values and faith. Christian singles' ministries can be very helpful in allow-ing us to build relationships with the opposite sex. I've been in our singles' group for more than ten years. It's embarrassing. I have the most tenure of anybody there. How "successful" of a singles' ministry can it be if I've been a member for that long and am still single? Fortunately, our ministry's focus isn't dat-ing but being complete in Christ. However, many are dating, but no one is asking me out. I'm not sure why. Maybe it's because I'm in leadership. I have resolved that when I com-plete my present leadership assignment, I'm taking a break. I'm gonna be a participant and get involved in a different ministry outside of my church. Most likely, though, God is just protect-ing me. He has things He wants me to do as a single. He wants me focused.

555 Singles Surveyed

Have You Used a Dating Service?

Men 17%

Women 10%

SWF seeking SWM for lasting relationship
25 y/o, brn hr/brn eyes, 5'7" n/s n/d, Christian, loves long walks

Of those who have used a dating service, 80% are twenty-eight or older.

Dana—I have a friend who met her husband through a type of dating service where they wrote letters back and forth. They are a wonderful couple and very happy. I see how it was an effec-tive tool in initiating the relationship. Though I am glad it worked for her, there is something about the setting up and not knowing part of the process that doesn't make me comfortable. And I have never gone, nor desire to go, on a blind date. It seems too stressful. I want to meet the person on my own. Yep, I want God to prepare me and drop someone in my lap. Is that so wrong?

I think the best way, initially, would be to get to know him in a group setting, without all the pressure. I'm definitely one who wants to have a solid friendship first. Some of my past relationships started off as dating and ended quickly. Enough of that. No thank you. I'd rather just hang out with a bunch of my friends.

Spending time with friends is comfortable and helps me to focus not on my lack of dates but instead on who I am as an individual, what I mean to my friends, and what they mean to me.

I also like to stay active and involved in different activities as a constructive way to utilize my time. Thankfully, service opportunities at our church are endless. In his ten years of serving as Singles Minister at East 91st Christian Street Church, Mark Wesner commented on the fulfillment singles find in serving the Lord together as a group or team: "Usually those that have their acts together and are confident are those individuals that are serving somehow. They are meeting people's needs. They are so caught up in being used by the Lord and being loved by those whom they serve that they don't even notice that they are not in a romantic relationship. It doesn't even occur to them. They may think about it occasionally, but they don't dwell on it."

Nathan—I can think of a couple of positive alternatives to the traditional form of dating. They center around "getting on with your life." First, work on service teams. The idea is to get involved, care about other people, do a good work, and get to know people of like mind, and maybe during the process you'll befriend someone and God will rap you on the head and say,

"Hey! There's the one. Wake up!" Second, work on yourself. I can't think of anyone who wants to spend time with a dull or spiritually underdeveloped person. Develop interests, get over that annoying habit, get hobbies that don't scare people away, read good books, get to know God's Word deeper, lead a Bible study, head up a ministry at church, get people involved in activities, and become a whole individual in God. I think working on yourself is the best thing to do to prepare for a boyfriend/girlfriend and ultimately a spouse. Think about it, they've got to spend time with you, so make it valuable for them. And if that person doesn't get put into your life, look what you've done for the Kingdom. That should be our first purpose, anyway.

If you've really gotta date, then you could join a Christian dating service. I'm not sure how prevalent they are, but I joined one in my town at one time. You get to meet as many people as you possibly can, and, since they are Christians, they should be open minded about meeting you. It's kind of interesting, like looking through the Sears catalog for that one special person.

There's also the non-Christian dating service. I joined one of those at an expense. I was new to town and I thought it would be a way to start meeting people. You must be very careful joining one of these because they are primarily interested in getting your money. Then, when you say you want to meet another Christian, they interpret it to mean someone who has been known to go to church from time to time. These didn't pan out for me; I immediately put my membership on hold because I was being fixed up by friends and family and meeting women at church. Then, one night, I saw a news investigation of this very dating service that revealed that a lot of criminals were making it through the screening process and into the fix-up files.

Be careful out there.

How to Find a Wife the Biblical Way

Today is a difficult time for the single, Christian man to date and follow God's will. Listed below are a few examples from the Bible of how some men found wives:

1. Find an attractive prisoner of war, bring her home, shave her head, trim her nails, and give her new clothes. Then she's yours. Israelites. (Deuteronomy 21:11–13)

2. Find a man with seven daughters, and impress him by watering his flock. Moses. (Exodus 2:16–21)

3. Purchase a piece of property, and get a woman as part of the deal. Boaz. (Ruth 4:5–10)

4. Go to a party and hide. When the women come out to dance, grab one and carry her off to be your wife. Benjamites. (Judges 21:19–25)

5. Have God create a wife for you while you sleep. Note: this will cost you a rib. Adam. (Genesis 2:19–24)

6. Agree to work seven years in exchange for a woman's hand in marriage. Get tricked into marrying the wrong woman. Then work another seven years for the woman you wanted to marry in the first place. That's right, fourteen years of toil. Jacob. (Genesis 29:15–30)

7. Cut the foreskins off 200 of your future father-in-law's enemies and get his daughter for a wife. David. (1 Samuel 18:27)

8. Even if supposedly no one is out there, just wander around a bit and you'll find someone. (Note: you may never get an explanation of where she came from.) Cain. (Genesis 4:16–17)

9. Find a prostitute and marry her. Hosea. (Hosea 1:1–3)

10. Become the emperor of a huge nation and hold a beauty contest. Xerxes/Ahasuerus. (Esther 2:3–4)

11. When you see someone you like, go home and tell your parents, "I have seen a woman; now get her for me." If your parents question your decision, simply say, "Get her for me. She's the one for me." Samson. (Judges 14:1–3)

12. Kill any husband and take his wife. Prepare to lose four sons, though. David. (2 Samuel 11)

13. Wait for your brother to die. Take his widow. It's not just a good idea, it's the law. Onan and Boaz. (Deuteronomy/Leviticus, example in Ruth)

14. Don't be so picky. Make up for quality with quantity. Solomon. (1 Kings 11:1–3)

15. A wife? . . . hmm . . . bad idea. Paul. (1 Corinthians 7:32–35)

Author unknown. Found on the Internet, June 1997. (Taken from *Single Adult Ministries Journal*, July/August 1997, p.1.)

Other Voices

Grover Levy—Worst-date scenarios for me are blind dates. I'm always a little uncomfortable. Actually I generally don't do them, as a rule. I'm just a little uncomfortable with that. I wouldn't say that they are horror stories, but you get out and you immediately realize you are not meant for each other. And then you're going to have to spend a couple of hours or more together.

Heather Floyd, Point of Grace—Dating shouldn't make you tired thinking about it. I respect a guy who lays it on the line even if I'm not interested. I respect him, and I'll respect him enough to tell him right out if I'm not interested. He deserves that respect.

Michael Passons, Avalon—Lots of old ladies try to fix me up with their daughters or their nieces. I have a strict policy: no blind dates. It's just too much of a strain, physically and emotionally, and I don't want to put myself through that. It's too nerve-wracking. I just cut them off. I used to try to be nice to the old ladies, but now I just say, "You know, I'm just not interested."

Cherie Paliotta, Avalon—If I had it to do all over again, I wouldn't have been in a serious, committed relationship until I had some idea of where I was heading. The problem with young people today is that they are getting intimately involved too early, and that's where you run into trouble. That's where the enemy will attack you. People forget to pray first. You just have to be really cautious. It's a definite discipline. You just really have to listen closely to the voice of God and pray about the decision you make.

The best way to meet someone is to get on your knees and

pray that God would bring him into your life, and He will, whether it be through the church, your job, or your friends or family. I'm speaking in faith because obviously He hasn't brought my husband into my life yet, but I believe that He will.

Grover Levy—It's very much okay for Christians to date; that's how you meet people; that's how you interact with people. If you don't date people, then it's kind of hard to know what you like in a woman. I think that's one of the great things about dating. It's good to date a lot of people, maybe a lot of different types of people, so you understand what it is you are looking for in a potential mate.

Rebecca St. James—I'm more into being friends with guys and going out in groups and getting to know people that way because I think it's much more real. You can be yourself when it's more relaxed. You're not staring across the table at somebody you totally don't know and trying to impress him by putting on an act when he's doing the same thing. Part of the reason I can see it that way is that my parents were best friends before they dated. My mom actually wouldn't date my dad until he got serious about God, so the relationship was very founded on Christ. That for me is just so important, making it founded on Jesus and making it also founded on friendship, that best friendship. So I'm just waiting on God's timing till He allows my best friend to come.

Rich Vincent, Singles Minister—Whether God provides a mate or not, that's another story. I do think though, if people do want to marry, then there are times when they should take some specific action steps to try to find a mate. I've encouraged people to use the Christian dating service before. I don't have any problem with that. Abraham sent his servant out to go find a date for

Isaac. What better place to look than in a good solid church or a Christian dating service? Here are two options: I could sit at home, or I could go to the Christian dating service. Is it sinful to sit at home? No. Is it sinful to use the dating service? No. So you have the freedom to do either and now you just say, "Lord, I commit my path to You, please bless it, please guide me in it."

Dr. John Trent, Encouraging Words—Dating should come out of Song of Solomon, chapter 1. You've got the courtship of Solomon and his bride. This is way before Solomon married hundreds of wives. There are some specific things in there. For example, the relationship is based on integrity. She starts off with: "May he kiss me with the kisses of his mouth! For your love is better than wine. Your oils have a pleasing fragrance, your name is like purified oil" (NASB). So there's a strong physical desire. So the point is it is great to have physical desires, but make sure it is based upon integrity. She starts off feeling very insecure but ends up feeling secure enough to say, "I'm the rose of Sharon."

That's the mark of real love. Are you getting more secure in a relationship, or do you feel less secure or less valued as a person? So pick somebody based on integrity. Let that be the thing that really lights your fire. Biblical love builds up.

Another principle in this chapter is that they dealt with small problems while they were small. That's really important in any relationship. She says, "Catch the foxes for us, the little foxes that are ruining the vineyard," which is a picturesque way of saying, "Solomon, we have some small problems. Now is the time to deal with them." If you are in a relationship with someone and they are unwilling to talk about or talk through issues, that's a real good indication that down the road things are gonna fail. So I think that courtship is a crucial part of marriage.

Geof Barkley—I realize that not all relationships will end up in marriage, but that is sort of the ideal ending. It is an objective of a dating person. As Christians we should be even more conscious of being respectful of whom we date and being respectful of honoring God with our dating lives, like the rest of our lives. Everything grows out of that Christian life. We don't apply Christianity to our lives; Christianity is our lives.

Jaci Velasquez—The church I go to is very into courtship instead of dating, and I'm really not. There are ways of dating that are the right way. But for people my age, the wisest way to be dating would be to go out and meet people through friends and hang out with them. I don't think dating is wrong, but you have to be wise in the way you choose your dates.

Rich Vincent, Singles Minister—Of course I say some pretty harsh things about "missionary dating" and the reason is, I've never seen it work except for one case. Because what happens is once your emotions get tied up, and you really are attracted to the person, then it becomes very easy to accept the lowest common denominator. You should realize the very first thing that ought to attract your future mate is the aspect of being a God-fearer, a Christian, someone who's really devoted to the Lord. That's the biggest mistake I see. The second biggest one is not treating each other as a brother and sister in Christ, by continuing to play the games rather than just being upfront—being willing to say, "I am interested in you." It seems like I run into this idea of it being a game. And don't get me wrong. There is something fun about the pursuit—there really is. I would never want to take that away.

Max Hsu, Church of Rhythm—A long, long, long, time ago, like last year, I was kind of looking for the one. I'd meet someone, and a little voice inside of me would say, "Are you the one?"

God brought me some light in that one. Instead of looking for a one or the one, I'm not really looking at all, but looking to God and trying to be friends with people. If anything is going to happen, it's gonna grow out of a friendship. I've always said that I want to marry my best friend, and I really hope, at the very least, that is what happens.

Do I Have Only One, One and Only?
"Are you the one?"

Lana—I don't think God has one person picked out for every one of us. I think for some He might have a particular person but only when it would help accomplish His purposes. Just as God might not have a chosen profession for everyone, for some He might. The only examples I recall from the Bible where God intervened in matchmaking efforts were with Rebecca and Isaac, with Mary and Joseph, and with Hosea and Gomer.

Nathan—There could be a best person for you to marry, but I think that the one you choose can become the best if you allow God to work within that situation. Romans 8:28 says that "in all things God works for the good of those who love him."

Rather than there being only one person for you, I think it's probably the right timing we should focus on. If you marry, there would have probably been numerous people with whom you could have made a godly life. It could be that you weren't suited for someone you knew in college, but now if you encounter him or her, the growth could have occurred that now allows you to be right for each other.

I think we should focus on patience and learn not to want anything in the wrong timing. That's a very tough thing. Ultimately we don't know if we are waiting on something from

God or if He even intends to give it to us. I hope we can be thankful for what God is doing in the here and now.

Dana—Instead of focusing on whether God has just one person for me, I think it is more helpful to pray that God would bless and enrich my friendships, realizing that it may very well be in His plan for me to stay single for the rest of my life. Desiring that not to be the case, though, my prayer for relationships in general has been to be involved in a healthy, God-centered relationship. I want to commit my life to a man who would be the spiritual leader of the relationship, have a true servant heart for God, strive to be obedient, not expect to change me, and love me as the Lord does—unconditionally. Okay. So I've been praying for the "perfect" guy. But why not? I think that the Lord knows me so well, and if He wants me to be married, He will have the best, most appropriate person for me. After all, I think He is somewhat qualified.

Chris—In a recent commercial, a guy missed a coincidental meeting with Ms. Right when his watch was set just seconds fast. That watchmaker would have us to believe that we get one chance at true love. I'm not so sure about that, and really I don't care too much. I can trust God that when the time is right He will allow me to cross the path of the one He has prepared for me.

Sometimes, though, I let myself wonder while I'm getting ready to go on a social outing if that night I'll meet "him." Each day I must be ready, for he may come at any time. It will probably be when I run to the grocery wearing sweats and thick glasses. God does have a sense of humor.

Other Voices

Greg Long—*If I have missed the one and my life is over, that's unfortunate. Certainly I don't want to live thinking that I've missed everything. Of the people I have dated in the last few* years, I think I could have married any of them. I wouldn't have gone wrong; I don't think there's just one person for you. I hope that it will work out fine someday. That's all I can say.

Max Hsu, Church of Rhythm—I used to be looking for my Holy Grail woman. And the thing that I think I learned this year is that it's more like flavors of ice cream. You just have to decide what flavor you want for the rest of your life. I think there are a couple of people I could marry, and it would work great. It's just that each one would have different things or characteristics about them.

I read somewhere, and this made a lot of sense to me, that when you get married God makes that person you marry the perfect person, because at that point, God put it together.

I read an article in Today's Christian Woman (and I read that because the associate editor is a really good friend of mine) that said there are bad people for you to marry, good people for you to marry, and perfect people for you to marry. And when you get married, if you marry someone in the good or perfect class, God makes them the perfect person for you.

When I get married, it will be God's will, and that person, the day we're married, will be the perfect person for me.

Janna Potter, Avalon—I'm not into making it happen. I think that if God has it planned, then it will happen. I just don't think, I've gotta get out there or I'm not going to meet the man intended to be my husband.

It may sound weird, and a lot of people don't do it, but you should be praying for your future spouse that God would prepare you and him for each other.

Rebecca St. James—I pray for my future husband. I ask God to give him wisdom in his decisions, to look after him, and to be his strength. I ask God to lead him, to guide him, and to prepare him for marriage (and prepare me for marriage). I think when you think like that and pray for the person, it just makes them more real and more like, "Wow. God has a plan, and He has the proper timing for this."

Nee-C Walls, Anointed—I think God has one chosen person for me. There is no way in the world that you could have a couple of people who would meet all my criteria. God desires us to be with one person first of all, so I do believe He has one special person for me and I'm gonna know who it is as soon I see this trait in him. When you go out with a guy and see a couple of traits that you like, you think, Well, maybe he could be it; maybe he is the one. Sometimes you look for those traits and they're not there. Then you're like, Alrighty then, he must not be the one.

Dennis Rainey, Family Life Today—I think with single people today there's far too much emphasis on finding the right person, rather than becoming the right person.

I've got a son who's single. He's a young single, but he's experiencing it. He's not married and all his friends are. I often quote Martin Lloyd-Jones, who said, "Faith is the refusal to panic." A lot of singles panic and settle for something other than God's best.

Jody McBrayer, Avalon—We've gotten into a little debate about this on the bus because the girls believe that everybody has his or her somebody. "You'll know it when it happens. It's magic." And it's not that I don't believe that, but I've just never experienced it.

Dick Purnell, Single Life Resources—Sometimes singles pray a lot and will be too spiritual. They'll pray a lot, and then, all of a sudden, they will meet someone who seems to fit whatever they prayed for and they'll fall like a ton of bricks. They'll say, "God's in this." And yet, they never even became friends. They don't even know the person.

I've had a guy tell me, "I know I am going to marry this girl." I asked him how he knew he was going to marry her. And the guy said, "God told me." I asked, "How did God tell you?" "I've been praying about it and God just told me." I asked, "How long have you dated this girl?" He said he never had a date with her. Wait a minute. "We're in the same church, and I've seen her. She's godly. That's what I want." Maybe it was his hormones. I think sometimes singles will overspiritualize the process.

Rich Vincent, Singles Pastor—I believe that we are to be guided by God's revealed will and not try to crystal-ball it. Number one: she should be a God-fearer. Number two: she should be willing to follow my leadership to some extent because I am supposed to lead her. Number three: she should have personality. Finally: we should have a physical attraction since that's mentioned in Song of Solomon. I think I could have found those four things in millions of Christian girls, at least thousands. So, before I married [my wife], I had the absolute privilege and freedom to decide which woman I wanted to commit myself to for life. But the moment that we said, "I do" I understood in retrospect—and that's the only way you can know God's will in specific matters—she was the one woman for me.

Pam Thum—An old Israeli custom believes there is one person—a soul mate—whom God ordained. But my God is a God of many chances, of resurrection and miracles, so I am not sure. . . .

Cherie Paliotta, Avalon—It's hard for me to tell because I can't see what's on the other side of the fence. But I think when the final chapter is closed, when God says, "Okay, now it's time," I know that he will be the one—the one who is the perfect complement for me.

Nee-C Walls, Anointed—I don't want somebody who will be in my shadow, but, instead, someone who has goals for himself. And the right person will not be worried about what's on the outside, but he will love me for the inside of me, whether I'm a size 2 or 26. And I would want him to love the Lord with all of his heart, because when he loves the Lord, he's going to know how to love me and we won't have major problems. He's still human, now, but you know.

Jeff Frankenstein, Newsboys—Other people say, "Oh, God has that perfect person for me, and someday he'll show up in shining armor." I think that's wrong. It creates a lot of false expectations, as if when that perfect person comes everything is supposed to be rosy, and there are not going to be any problems or difficulties, and you won't have to build up a relationship because that will just be the perfect person and everything will be perfect. I think people get misled.

I believe that He can bring people into your path. But ultimately it is up to you to make the effort. I don't think there's one predestined, chosen person. That's where Christian singles get into trouble.

Jody McBrayer, Avalon—I believe God's will is that we obey Him and love Him. I don't believe God says that we only have one specific person.

I don't think that if we stub our toe on the sidewalk before we get to the corner and miss seeing someone that we have necessarily missed the one we are intended to marry. I don't think life is that way. There are many people who could work.

But God knows the future, so He knows the person that you will meet. If you look at it later in hindsight, yes, God gave you that one person, but right now it's not so clear.

Grover Levy—I think that there could probably be any number of people whom a person could marry. I think it's just a matter of finding somebody whom you feel comfortable with and whom you feel like God has released you to marry, and then just sticking with it. But I don't necessarily believe that there is only one person out there for you.

Who Asks? Who Pays?
"I like the sweet, old-fashioned ways."

Lana—I used to ask guys out. I would get frustrated that things weren't happening. I would get tired of waiting and then make the first move. I don't think this is necessarily wrong. However, I don't think it's best either. I want someone who is crazy about me and willing to pursue me. He would be confident enough in himself to take a risk. I shouldn't need to try to pursue him. Call it following "The Rules," but I think it's right on the money. For those who are lacking the courage to ask me out, I'm praying they will find their nerve.

The older I get, the more I like the traditional dating approach. At the beginning of the relationship, I want the man to pay. I don't like it when the guy suggests we split the check on the first date. When we have gone out for a while, I'll invite him over and make him dinner. Then as our relationship progresses, I think it's fine for me to pay. Dating certainly isn't cheap, and I am capable of sharing the expense. In fact, sometimes I am uncomfortable if a guy spends a lot on me.

Nathan—Whoever asks, pays. Period. They should write it into law. Women have gotten themselves into the situation that it is okay for them to ask men out, so they should also be willing to pay And I think they are. I think that the asker is the payer until a solid relationship is established. So then, when you've been dating for a year and your girlfriend says, "Let's see a sobby movie this Friday," she's not asking you out. She is suggesting that since you are probably going to be together, this is what she wants to do. So you, as the attentive boyfriend, go and buy discount tickets at your place of employment so that you can "be the man" and pay for the evening's outing. And if your place of employment doesn't have this benefit, get another job. Once in a while she will say, "You've been so good and have not been late coming by this month, and I want to take you out for ribs." Then you know that she is paying, but you should offer to leave the tip because "you-the-man." Even when you are being treated, chivalry should remain in a Christian relationship and you should at least slap a couple of bills onto the table to demonstrate that your desire is to take care of her (even if she makes twice your income). The point isn't that women need to be taken care of; it's that you demonstrate that you are happiest when you give.

This is not a self-help, how-to book, but I just thought I would offer a little instruction here: I think the only time you can be okay not offering the tip is on your birthday when she is totally taking care of you.

Chris—I'm one of the old-fashioned girls. He should ask, and he should pay. It's always awkward, though. The check comes. We both look at it lying there face down, but we try not to let the other see our glance. Do I reach for my purse to show my willingness, or do I just sit there, expecting him to pay?

I've known guys who were offended by my offer to treat, while I've known others who graciously accepted my offer to help.

We women, with our liberation and determined independence, have left men in confusion and heightened sensitivity. Do we want our doors opened? Is it okay if he pays? Do we mind him assuming control over the date? The answers are yes, yes, and no. Women want to be cared for—at least, I do.

555 Singles Surveyed

Is It Okay for a Woman to Ask a Man for a Date?

Among Women Surveyed,
54% *said "Okay"*

Among Men Surveyed,
80% *said "Okay"*

Dana—I don't really have a problem with girls asking guys out, but I wouldn't do it. Just as guys do, gals have to have some sense that the response will be positive. I guess the going-out part would have to be defined. Is this an official date? A lunch meeting? A companion to a wedding? I think it all depends on the situation. If it's a casual outing with a friend, or a movie with a group of people, then yeah, fine. There's no pressure for either person. But with an actual asking-out-to-dinner on a Friday or Saturday night, I would expect the guy to do the asking. Sure, gals are often going to initiate a phone call, but when it comes to a real date, I think that should be left up to the guy. And if he wanted to ask me out officially, it would be nice for him to pay for the meal, but I would never completely expect it. In less formal settings, though—lunch, popcorn at movies, ice cream, dessert cafés—I always like to split the cost. It doesn't seem right for him to pay for everything. Helping to pay keeps things casual. The emphasis is on being together and having a great time without pressure for the guy to pick up the tab. When he pays, it just seems more serious.

Other Voices

Max Hsu, Church of Rhythm—Almost all my girlfriends approached me after being friends for a while and said, "I'd like to date you." And I said, "Oh, that's where we were going?"

I used to think that I needed to lead the relationship, but this year I've had my butt kicked. I think a partnership is what it should be. A good balance is great. If I feel like I have to lead, I can miss things that are really important.

Cherie Paliotta, Avalon—If you are a Christian and you love the Lord and your main motivation is serving God, then you don't want to be with a person whom you have to try to pull into the Kingdom. As a woman, you don't want to have to be the spiritual leader in that relationship. That is not the way God designed it. I have been in that before, and it is a very discouraging thing. It's not my place, it's not my job, and it's not what God has called me to be. I'm supposed to be the spiritual helpmate, not the leader.

Geof Barkley—[A girl asking me out] is no big deal. I appreciate honesty. If a girl is interested enough to say, "I'd like to go out," then I've got no problem with that. Since she is being honest, if I'm not interested, I'll be honest enough to let her know.

Michael Passons, Avalon—I don't see anything wrong with [girls asking]. If the guy's interested, he'll say yes. If he likes aggressive women, then he knows exactly what he's getting.

Jo Ann Anderson, Singles Minister—As a woman, I never wanted to pursue a man because if I did, there would always be a doubt in my mind. Was he really interested in me? Or did he go out with me because I pursued him? *I would want to know that the man was initiating. Also, if a man cannot initiate and pursue me, I can't really respect him. That's a part of masculinity. You are confident in yourself as a man, you have enough esteem to pursue a woman, and you make yourself vulnerable to say, "I'm interested in you. Will you go out with me?" That really follows the natural order. I don't think it's a sin if girls ask guys out, but I would want to know that he was man enough to pursue me.*

Rebecca St. James—I can't speak for anyone else, but I don't think I would do it. I'm a bit of a romantic, and I like the sweet, old-fashioned ways: slowly getting to know each other, hanging out a bit more, and him eventually having the courage to say, "Would you like to come meet my family?" I think that would be the greatest thing for a guy to say: "Come hang out at my house with my siblings and my parents. Come have a meal at our house." That would be just beautiful.

Heather Floyd, Point of Grace—It's not easy being the only single in Point of Grace, especially at awards ceremonies or dinners that we all have to go to. Everybody has husbands there. My roommate said, "Why not take this guy to the Doves this year?" And I said, "I don't know if I want to take anybody." Why should I take someone just to have someone to be there by my side? I'm not dating him. I'm not in love with him. There's no reason to have someone next to me unless it is someone I want to go with. I don't want to have someone just to fill that space. They do have seat fillers at the Dove Awards.

Gary Mullet—I know my folks wouldn't like [girls asking], but I have no problem with it. To me anything that could eliminate guesswork is great, none of this cat and mouse business.

Jaci Velasquez—I don't feel weird asking a guy to do lunch, to go to a function with me, or to see a movie. I am nothing like my family. My mother would never do that in a million years, and my dad thinks it's completely unbelievable. He would never want me to do that. But with all the guys I know, I am just their friend. We just hang out.

Pam Thum—I'm probably a very old-fashioned girl that way. If you've been friends for a while, and if you're casual it's okay, but not, "I'd like to officially ask you out on a date, and I'll pick you up at this time." I'll let the guys do that.

Nee-C Walls, Anointed—I think a woman who [asks men out] intimidates them because they are pushed out of their leadership role. They don't feel like the man in the relationship, and it also makes the girl look very needy and very desperate.

The Perfect Date
"The moonlight would reflect off the carriage as he arrives . . ."

Lana—I think my ideal date depends on where I am in the dating process and how I feel about the person. One guy took me to a romantic restaurant with violinists walking around our table. It seemed like he would propose any moment, but it was only our first date. It was too much for me at that stage.

My ideal "first date" would be dinner and maybe a walk. I met one man through the Christian singles' dating service. We met for dinner downtown and then just walked around, checking out the shops and talking. It was great.

555 Singles Surveyed

How Many Dates Have
You Had This Month?

None	57%
1 or 2	22%
3 to 5	11%
5 to 10	4%
10+	6%

Chris—Some mystery would be nice: he could call and tell me what to wear and what time to be ready. From then on, he would line up all we'd do. Surprise and mystery are romantic. My idea of a great date is when I feel like we have really communicated. Movies are bad dates because you don't get to know each other; you just sit and stare at a screen. But sometimes it is nice after a long dinner to see a movie. It gives you the opportunity to cuddle.

A picnic in the park would be awesome. My date would bring his guitar and play a little, then we'd read from a book together. We might canoe or hike a little. We'd share from our hearts, we'd laugh, and we'd hold hands as we walked and talked. Okay, maybe I'm trapped in a dream world, but this dream is in color.

Dana—My ideal date would be with my best friend—someone I would not be embarrassed to eat those messy sandwiches with lingering lettuce in front of.

If I could set the stage, we would both be dressed nicely—formal, but comfortable—and we would dine at an outdoor restaurant overlooking the water. The meal would taste home-cooked, maybe with some grilled items, and we would eat, talk a little, and laugh a lot. We might even share some dessert before standing up to have a dance. Eventually, he would take me back to my house, walk me to the door, and give me a warm smile and a long hug. Hugs are great. Especially hugs from your best friend.

Nathan—Okay, first of all I would write a Shakespearean-style sonnet with correct meter and structure to read to her while we sat beside an English countryside brook. Salisbury Cathedral would be in the background, and we would savor juicy pomegranates. She'd be wearing lace, and I would be in a top hat.

That's what it sounds like most of you women want. I think you're all basing your ideas of ideal dates on Jane Austen novels.

I think if you're blessed enough to have a date that goes well and you have both enjoyed the company, you should consider it an ideal date. That mutual "like" is hard enough to find.

I remember one time, my girlfriend and I rode the train in from the suburbs of Chicago to downtown with her family. After we all had a late lunch, her family went back home, and we strolled around the city and visited Navy Pier. Then, in the evening, we rode the train through the night to get home, stopping once to share a bagel. It seemed ideal because a train was involved. Something about trains always boosts the romantic factor. It was getting late, it was she and I, just taking our time and enjoying the ride.

Another time, I took her to dinner in downtown Chicago for Christmas. We exchanged gifts and took a walk down by the Lincoln Park Zoo. It should have been icy and freezing, but it was a calm night, and we walked and walked.

Other Voices

Jeff Frankenstein, Newsboys—I love being adventurous and try-ing different foods. I think going to see the symphony is always a great date. To me a good date isn't exactly what you do. It can be just having good communication and having fun. What you do is not what makes it good; it's connecting with the person you're with.

Max Hsu, Church of Rhythm—Guys don't like to share this stuff. We get so busted. Because if you have one or two things you always do, then you're so busted if you try to use them again.

Heather Floyd, Point of Grace—I'm a big romantic. I like for a guy to plan the entire evening down to the last detail. You know that he is thinking of you the entire time through each detail, all just to please you.

Grover Levy—Best dates: those are usually the ones where you're just hanging out. You don't even have to go do anything except maybe dinner and a movie. Sometimes the best dates are just going to the bookstore and looking around or just taking a walk around the lake or around the park or whatever. Basically it's a cool date if you really dig being with that person. It does not matter what you do.

Geof Barkley—Ideal date? I'm so uncreative, so inadequate. Bulls game, I don't know.

It wouldn't have to be any particular place, but it would be a person I really enjoy being with, and it would have to be a comfortable atmosphere. By the end of the night, I would think, Gosh, where did the time go?

Gary Mullet—My best dates have been where you're so comfortable with each other and you start talking, and all of a sudden you look over at the clock and it's 2:00 in the morning. That to me is the coolest.

The Unusual, the Embarrassing, and the Unexpected
"How 'bout them Bears."

Lana—I went to a formal dance where my date and I doubled with my girlfriend and her date. Unfortunately, we didn't compare notes. My girlfriend and I wore the same dress, and the guys each wore brown suits. We looked like a singing group.

Chris—Living with four brothers could have been more embarrassing for me, I guess. They usually were pretty good. But once in a while, when a guy called, they would get a big smile on their face. With the phone not far from their mouth, they'd yell, "Hurry, Chris, it's a *man!*"

Dana—It was a sunny, beautiful day from what I could tell from my office window, and I decided it might be nice if my friend met me for lunch at a deli just minutes from work. Knowing how coworkers jump at the chance to tease me about my dating life, I tried not to act too excited about the "lunch date" in five minutes with the well-dressed, striking man who would drive up in his shiny red convertible. I hoped no one would notice my excitement or my urgency to wrap up my last call before lunch and head out the door.

We drove to the deli and found a table just outside the restaurant. We sat down and started talking. I was laughing and enjoying his company, when I just happened to look up and to my left. Shocked, I saw two of the sales reps from work standing inside the large restaurant window, nearly pressed up against the glass, with these wide, toothy, happy grins. It was almost as if they thought they had caught me or something. They stood there, hands rapidly waving back and forth in excitement. They were practically gawking at us, and there I was trying not to react.

Nathan—I think just going on a first date is an embarrassing moment. It's usually the night when the wind blows my hair so that there's one chunk standing up for the whole evening, and I don't even know it until I get home and look in the mirror. It's usually when I'm thinking, *That went smoothly and I think she likes me. I'll call her tomorrow.* Then, I peer into the mirror and behold: *She'll never go out with me again.* I have a

---

Best Pickup Line Comebacks

I know how to please a woman.
Then please leave me alone.

I want to give myself to you.
Sorry, I don't accept cheap gifts.

Your hair color is fabulous.
Thank you. It's on aisle three at the corner drugstore.

You look like a dream.
Go back to sleep.

I can tell that you want me.
Yes, I want you to leave.

Hey, baby, what's your sign?
Stop.

I'd go through anything for you.
Let's start with your bank account.

May I have the last dance?
You've just had it.

Your place or mine?
Both. You go to your place, and I'll go to mine.

Your body is like a temple.
Sorry, there are no services today.

Is this seat empty?
Yes, and this one will be too if you sit down.

What's it like being the most beautiful girl here?
What's it like being the biggest liar in the world?

Haven't I seen you someplace before?
Yeah, that's why I don't go there anymore.

Author unknown. Found on the Internet.

picture from a high school dance with that one chunk of hair sticking up. Why couldn't my date have told me about it before the picture?

Lana—On one date, the guy suggested going to his house and reading Mark Twain. I couldn't imagine this, especially for a first date. I also couldn't comprehend how we would do this. Did he have two books? Would he read to me and then I to him? Would we read the same book at the same time? It was too different for me. We agreed, instead, to go out to eat and catch a video with my roommate and her boyfriend. As we were looking for the video, he'd ask me if I had seen a particular movie. I'd say "yes," and then he would proceed to tell me everything about the video even though I had seen it. That was our last date.

Dana—One day I took a boyfriend to my parents' home so he could get to know my family. Aside from brief, casual meetings, this was the first time he and I had attempted to spend some quality time with my parents. As a popular after-dinner event, we all gathered around the card table for some serious competition. During one hand, the game became very tense, and when my boyfriend played the winning card, the frustration sparked a reaction: Dad flicked the side of his head. Whap! Time stopped for a moment as my mom, brother, and I all looked at my boyfriend and then at Dad and back to my boyfriend. When we realized what had happened, we broke out in disbelieving laughter. Even though we knew my dad to be quite the character at times, we all couldn't believe how he just felt so inclined to "flick" our new guest. And Dad couldn't believe it either. That's what made it even funnier. Mom and I, with our nurturing side surfacing, apologized for Dad, but we couldn't help but laugh at my boyfriend's "initiation."

Chris—My first real car date was exciting. My date and I were going to Denny's for dinner on a cold January evening. In the parking lot we realized that the doors weren't going to open. We rolled down the windows and got out the "Dukes of Hazard" way. He was so embarrassed; I just thought it was funny.

Nathan—I've gone through a ton of fix-ups. Let's see, there was the one girl who seemed very career-oriented and self-sufficient on the first date but, on the second date, told me of every dumping she had suffered through and several engagement break-ups. By the third month, she was telling me that she needed a man to run her life. We broke it off at Christmas. There was the fix-up who would agree to a date one night, but when I called the day of the date to confirm, she would claim she had to clean her whole apartment that night. After two of these episodes, I realized it was never happening. We had never met face-to-face. What? Did she think I was stupid? Then there was the fix-up with the teacher back at my old high school. I thought, *There's at least a starting point for conversation. I graduated from that school, and she is teaching there.* We met at a school function. I was happy to know she was close to her students. But when she allowed them to whisper in her ear, look at me, and giggle, and then she herself did the same thing, I thought, *This is sick. I'm not in high school anymore.* And since I don't take well to being talked about in front of my face and laughed at, I said, "It was nice meeting you" and walked away. It was odd that it turned out that way. I'm not overly goofy-looking.

Other Voices

Heather Floyd, Point of Grace—I just don't like to date shorter guys. I'm 5'10". In college, I went to a movie with this guy, and we had our arms on the armrest. He wanted to hold my hand.

But my arm was so much longer than his arm. My hand was all bent back. It was the most awkward thing.

Gary Mullet—I made a reservation at this really swank restaurant, really nice. I'm getting ready before I go pick up this girl, shaving, just taking my time, and the phone rings. She asks, "Where are you?" I'm like, "What are you talking about? I'm shaving. I'm getting ready to pick you up. I'll be there in about a half-hour." Something had happened to the clock. I was already an hour and a half late to pick her up. I called the restaurant and asked could we please still get in there. And they set a table aside for us. We're driving over. She's so upset, I'm upset, and we're not talking. We're driving along about 80 mph and we hit this dog, and kapow! I can't even describe it. We both just about started crying. Oh, it was horrible. That was a bad night.

Max Hsu, Church of Rhythm—A girl I had been interested in called me. She had moved, and she said, "I'm gonna be in town. Do you want to get together?" I said, "Oh, cool, I'd love to get together." I thought it would be her and me. So I get there, and it is her and her new boyfriend. And then not only that, but the guy she dated before me showed up too. So now there are four of us. Then she goes to the bathroom. Then it is me and these other two guys whom I really don't know at all, and our common interest is this girl who's now in the bathroom. Then it was like, "Yeah, how 'bout them Bears." What do you talk about?

Heather Floyd, Point of Grace—I had been seeing this guy. We had gone out several times. I just kept thinking that he wanted to kiss me. He had this look in his eyes, you know. I thought, Maybe he is too shy. I kept thinking, I know he wants to kiss me. Maybe he was too scared because he knows who I am and knows that I stand for sexual purity. *Maybe he doesn't want to mess that up, as if kissing would.* Well, he wants to kiss me, and I want to kiss him. *So we're getting out of the car. We were standing there talking. It was awkward. So I kissed him. I just went for it. We kissed for a minute. And afterward he goes, "I normally don't kiss this early in a relationship."* I thought, Okay, I was reading you all wrong. Okay, what am I? I'm Miss Aggressive here.

Staying Pure
"Pursue God's way. Don't even mess with any other."

Nathan—I'm going to sound like I'm preaching to people, but I'm in the congregation too. Even once you've gotten into a secure relationship that is lasting, I can't think of anything beyond kissing that is okay. You're not married, even if you're engaged. Kisses, hugs—they're okay if you know your limits of self-control. If passionate kissing begins leading somewhere else, you should establish boundaries. Remember, before we are married, no matter how passionately in love we are, God considers us sisters and brothers and we should treat each other accordingly. First Timothy 5:1–2 says, "Treat younger men as brothers, older women as mothers, and younger women as sisters, with absolute purity."

Loneliness is no excuse for falling into premarital sex. It can be easy, but it's still no excuse. We think television and movies make it hard for us. If they do, then we should turn them off. We should know the Word more than anything, and there shouldn't be any gray areas for us. When we fall, when we look at things we shouldn't have looked at, we should pray for forgiveness, ask God to rebuke Satan for tempting us, and pray for strength and wisdom. Like our singles pastor taught, find a verse concerning the temptation plaguing you and quote it as soon as the suggestion arises. Then ask God to rebuke Satan. It's powerful. Satan eventually gets very afraid and we develop power over the sin that used to enslave us. There is nothing that will make you more excited about being a child of God than when you begin realizing that all power is yours and Satan is already defeated.

Everybody suffers the same sorts of temptation—married, divorced, widowed, single. We are all in the same race to the end. We cannot set ourselves apart simply because we have single status and say that it is harder for us and then slide into a death spiral. Pray, pray, pray.

Lana—Because I became a Christian in high school, I have been spared a lot of heartbreak because I decided to stay sexually pure until I get married. However, I didn't expect to be a thirty-five-year-old virgin. I feel like an endangered species, a real phenomenon. Honestly, I am almost embarrassed to say that I am a virgin. Isn't that sad?

I remember going to the doctor for what I thought was an infection. The doctor said that I could be pregnant. I said that I couldn't. She kept insisting that I could. Finally, I said, "Doesn't that require sex?" She said, "Well, yes, it does." "Then I couldn't be pregnant!" Unfortunately, in our society, it is assumed that you are sexually active. If you are not, the next assumption is that you are gay. Rarely do people consider that you just may be abstaining.

I hope I get married before Christ returns and am able to experience a sexual relationship. That way in heaven if someone says, "This is better than sex," I'll have something for comparison.

In Spanish, "Lana" means wool. I once had a coat that said "100% Virgin Lana," which, of course, was true. I gave the coat to my sister. I didn't want it to become a self-fulfilling prophecy.

I want to experience sex, but I want to experience it when I am married and it is part of the greater love picture. This man will love me, and I will love him. If I go ahead and have sex now, I'll be cheating myself out of the joy of what I'll have when I am married. I know this is true in my head. Sometimes, it's a little more difficult to convince the rest of me. And, unfortunately, sometimes it's even more challenging to explain to the men I am dating.

God calls me to stay sexually pure. It's not that strange actually if I keep my focus on godly things. I've been told time and time again by my married friends that it's worth the wait. I'm committed to waiting. It's just that all our culture seems to be obsessed with the sexual experience, and I sometimes feel left out. I'm also not sure the rest of my body always knows that I am single.

I would like to be able to relate better to God's love. God compares His love for us with the love between a husband and wife and the love of a parent for his child. I've never experienced either of these types of love.

There are other issues of purity that affect me. What's my biggest struggle? Is it TV, movies, or books? Actually, it's the Internet. I found myself browsing where I should never have gone. It started out frankly as curiosity, seeing some pictures and reading some stories, and then it moved to my thoughts and desiring to go back and be curious some more. James 1:14 and 15 says: "But each one is tempted when he is carried away and enticed by his own lust. Then when lust has conceived, it gives birth to sin; and when sin is accomplished, it brings forth death" (NASB). I must take every thought captive. To help me stay pure in searching the Internet, I put Philippians 4:8,

"Whatever is true, whatever is honorable, whatever is right, whatever is pure . . . let your mind dwell on these things" (NASB), on my computer desktop. When I get tempted to browse to those areas, I see that verse. I leave the computer and try to go do something different, like prepare my lesson for Bible Study Fellowship. That always works. It's hard to keep thinking impure thoughts when I'm reading the cleansing Word of God.

555 Singles Surveyed

Concerning Sexual Purity

96% *Believe in Abstinence*

89% *of those who said they didn't believe in abstaining said they were Christians.*

Dana—When God commands us to lead a life of purity and holiness, He means just that. He doesn't say that we can create our own rules for living. Sometimes I can rationalize things, trying to fool myself into thinking my way is in line with what the Lord has for me.

I know I have to be grounded in the Word. I can't for a minute think that I am strong enough or that I won't get into a potentially tempting situation. I don't want to do anything that is not pleasing to God. It's silly to think I can hide from the Lord. He knows everything. He knows even if I have the slightest impure thought. I have to remind myself that the Lord is literally right there with me.

The Lord intends for us to be holy and regard our body as His temple. The Word is clear on this issue: "The body is not meant for sexual immorality, but for the Lord, and the Lord for the body . . . Flee from sexual immorality. All other sins a man commits are outside his body, but he who sins sexually sins against his own body. Do you not know that your body is a temple of the Holy Spirit, who is in you, whom you have received from God? You are not your own; you were bought at a price. Therefore honor God with your body" (1 Corinthians 6:13, 18–20).

These words remind me that even though we are human, there is no gray area to consider according to what He has for us. And although He will forgive us when we repent for our sins, that can't be an excuse. We can't take advantage of Him and use that grace as a green light to sin again. A friend once told me an analogy where there is a small stain on one white cloth and a large stain on another white cloth. Although one stain is obviously bigger and more noticeable, the small stain is just as apparent against the white cloth; it has damaged the cloth as well. And just as a stain is a stain, so too is a sin a sin. It doesn't matter how big or small the sin may seem, in God's eyes, it's just as harmful. I've learned that when I sin in any way, I not only hurt myself, but I hurt the Lord. Every time I sin, I disappoint Him. All I ever want to do is honor Him with my life. That is so convicting.

Chris—God has certainly protected me in this area. When I was sixteen, dating an eighteen-year-old, I would have done anything for him. He's the one who would stop us when we got too physical. He was a strong Christian, and, since I came from a non-Christian family, I learned a lot about faith from him. We had an on-again, off-again relationship for two years, and I never quite knew where I stood. I think I was trying to win him over. In my insecurity, I would totally trust him to decide when to stop, or maybe it was that I didn't care. He was important to me, and I wanted to prove it to him. He was a volunteer firefighter, and we would hang out at the firehouse alone. It was God or fate that would make an alarm go off just when our make-out sessions were heating up.

God kept me from dating guys who would pressure me. He allowed me to break up with those who wanted more than I wanted to give. And He offered grace when the line would be crossed.

But it's pretty weird to say that I'm only a few months shy of thirty and still a virgin. I live in a different world. In this day, though, it is so difficult to be truly pure. I know a lot about the subject from TV, movies, and hearing people—even my students—talk. Sometimes I wonder if God wanted me to be more clueless, more pure until my wedding night about such things. The stuff I allow to invade my mind affects the purity I want to offer my husband someday. There's so much more to purity than not being sexually active.

As I push the boundaries of how far I can go and allow thoughts, words, and pictures to take residence in my mind, I lose some freshness, some innocence. I lose some of the purity that was meant as a gift from God and as my gift back to God. Instead of the clean, white sheet of paper I wanted to give my future spouse to write on, will I guardedly hand him a dingy, crumpled sheet? It only has a few scribbles here and there, but its beauty was sacrificed, its purpose cheapened. Can I be proud that it stayed *mostly* white? Or that it isn't torn, only crumpled?

God can renew our purity. He forgives and forgets. We are the ones who will struggle to let go of the past. If we only ask, God gives us a fresh start, a new crisp sheet of paper. But will I protect it better today than yesterday?

Other Voices

Jeff Frankenstein, Newsboys—I think our generation is just totally distracted. I look at singles in other countries who are so focused on God and their relationship with Christ. In other countries they don't watch cable TV or call 900 numbers and all this stuff here. We're just constantly distracted. The main thing is to set time aside to be focused on why we're here on the earth and what we're here to do and not to be distracted.

Heather Floyd, Point of Grace—Just about everything in our society makes it harder on our purity. We need accountability—more than just one person too. Even the strongest Christian person is weak. I don't care who they are. I know I am weak. And God has protected me.

We were in the hotel the other day and I was flipping through channels. HBO has this show about sex. I had never seen it before and I didn't know what it was. I stopped there for a minute, and I had to make my finger turn the channel. What was on there was appalling, but it was so appalling that I wanted to watch it. But I knew that once I watched it then my thoughts would be there. And that's just not good. So, once you think of God in that situation, you are like, just turn it off. I don't have to watch any TV.

Rich Mullins—Chastity is learning how to love purely, how to love without possessing, how to love without controlling, how to love without expecting love back.

Cherie Paliotta, Avalon—God created men and women to desire each other, and it's a beautiful thing when it's in its right place and in the right timing—under the umbrella of marriage. It's a blessing. But sometimes we, in our own situation, will take the initiative to move faster than God wants us to.

Rebecca St. James—In concert every night I share a note a lady wrote to me about premarital sex:

"My whole adult life is the result of premarital sex and going on to marrying the wrong man. We even had an abortion then divorced. On and on it's gone, so I don't want my two daughters to follow 95 percent of my footsteps. I can't even hold down a job. I thought of speaking to youth groups about the wrongness of premarital sex. I thought that these men cared about me. I felt popular and accepted. Boy, was I mistaken. I pay the price of my sin often."

I use this lady's honesty and her experience as a way to say to pursue God's way. Don't even mess with any other.

Dennis Rainey, Family Life Today—I think singles are looking for hope concerning relationships. I think they're scared to death. And I think what we present day in and day out on our broadcast is a call to holiness, a call to right relationships. And I think singles, for the most part, are hungry to hear that standard. We need to challenge them back to the standard. You ought to hear the phone calls we get when we challenge single people. Their lives have been horribly compromised. It's because they've not been reminded of what the standard is: 2 Corinthians 7:1 tells us to lay aside everything and press on toward holiness. There are a lot of heartaches, a lot of hurts, and a lot of needs in the single community.

Nee-C Walls, Anointed—Some people get to the point while they are in that waiting period, they faint and they die because they've given in and settled for something they really didn't have to settle for because they just get impatient and just can't wait. But it's good to wait. Patience is a virtue. Love is patient, and love is kind. So when you get into a relationship with that guy and he wants to go a little bit further, tell him to wait. He will wait if he really loves you.

Pam Thum — I've come to this conclusion from my mistakes, but I'd say the perfect way to date is to be friends, go out and talk and pray, but skip the physical. I think for me that kisses mean something. I think too many people throw them away. The guys too. That doesn't mean the person you kiss is the person you're going to marry; that's unrealistic in this world. The ideal would be to really get the friendship going, get to know the families, have fun, and pray about your situation. Then, when you know it's right, you can start holding hands and kissing.

Mitch McVicker — I try to focus on the lust of the eyes because Jesus warned that it is as bad as committing adultery. This was set up for us because lusting in your inner soul starts you down the road to something that couldn't be good for us. It's like brushing your teeth. If you don't brush your teeth, you'll have to face the consequences of your teeth rotting out.

Celibacy is to avoid sexual immorality. It can steer you from something very big coming down the line. God tries to keep our hearts and souls protected until they can be fully expressed.

Geof Barkley — We are to be in the world and not of the world. I think sometimes as Christians we let down our guard. You get involved. You let down your guard and before you know it you slip into the rut, watching a few more movies, catching a little more TV, and listening to more music. It's everywhere. You really have to keep your guard up and keep your relationship with Christ in the center of things.

Jaci Velasquez—I think that sexual purity is definitely the most difficult struggle of them all. I believe that this is one of the most important fights to go through because this is the one fight that God's really gonna bless you with and honor you with.

Jody McBrayer, Avalon—The only way we can understand true love is to understand God's love. Especially with guys, sex is such an important thing, a status symbol. But with our relationship with Christ, I want a quality love. You can't find it except through Jesus.

Jo Ann Anderson, Singles Minister—I know women who have been Christians for more than twenty years who are distraught because they are still virgins. They see being a virgin as a black mark on their record, a confirmation that they are undesirable. I personally view virginity as an incredible blessing in our day, something to be guarded and treasured. Prior to my decision to follow Christ, I was not sexually pure, and it was the biggest disgrace in my life. If there were anything that I could take back today, it would be my virginity.

When I talk with these women, I ask them, "What are you thinking? Do you understand all that goes along with losing your virginity?" The tragedy is that they don't understand because society and the media are glamorizing sexual relationships outside marriage and convincing people that there is something wrong with them as a person if this sexual element is missing from their life. What a tragic, life-altering lie.

Having the "We-Gotta-Talk" Talk
"I just want to be friends."

Lana—If I am going to end a relationship or someone ends one with me, I like doing it over the phone. Breaking up in person is too hard for me, especially if I'm being the one dumped. I think the phone allows more dignity. Now, if it's a very serious relationship, that definitely has to be done in person.

My hardest breakup was during my senior year in college. My boyfriend and I had only been dating for about two months when he had to quit school to take care of his family. Soon after, he told me that he was in love with me and wanted to know how I felt. I wasn't sure of my feelings. So much had happened and another male friend in our Bible study had started telling me that he cared for me. When my boyfriend finally put me on the spot, I said that I wanted to continue seeing him, but, at that time, I didn't think I loved him. He was really hurt. I think with all the tragedy in his life, it was too much. About a month later, I realized that I did in fact love him. We kept seeing each other, and I tried to assure him of my love, but it was too late. He ended our relationship. I regret that I wasn't more certain of my feelings. What really bothers me is that a couple of years later, when I called him just to say hello, he wouldn't take my call.

Dana—In one particular case, I knew that the official breakup was soon to happen, I just didn't know when. The two of us rang in the New Year with my college roommate and her husband. We had a nice dinner, went to a fairly entertaining New Year's party, and reminisced about our college days. We seemed to be having a nice time until the three-hour drive home. We argued a bit, discussed our "concerns," and tried to find some sort of resolution, but we both knew we weren't getting anywhere.

The next time I saw him, we went to a movie that was very funny—but the joke was on me. He broke it off during lunch over fries and burgers. The famous line, "I just want to be friends." How nice. Go to the movies, come back with no date, no relationship. At least we actually are friends now; we write at least once a year. Sometimes friends just need to stay friends.

Another relationship didn't end so smoothly. I guess you don't have to be a rocket scientist to realize it's not too bright to date a nonbeliever. What was I thinking? The yoke wasn't even close to being equal. I was compromising my faith. Second Corinthians 6:14 says, "Do not be yoked together with unbelievers. For what do righteousness and wickedness have in common? Or what fellowship can light have with darkness?" I found out the hard way that the answers to these questions were "nothing" and "none."

Chris—Dan went away to Mexico for the summer on a mission trip. We wrote a little, but I was on a mission trip in Michigan, so neither of us had a lot of time. When he was to arrive home, I drove three hours to his mom's house and waited with her when he got off the bus. I wanted to surprise him. I was so excited. As he got off the bus, his face couldn't hide that he wasn't happy to see me. He looked very depressed and barely talked to his mom or me that night. I got up early and left the next day. He never called.

Back at college two weeks later, we were on the same leadership team for a Christian organization. We had to attend the same retreat before school started. He wouldn't even look at me. Everyone noticed the difference in him. For about two months, he avoided me every time we had to be together. Every possible scenario went through my mind that took me through the gamut of emotions.

He showed up at my door one day in the late fall, saying that he owed me an explanation. Really?

We sat for a few minutes in silence before he started. He explained that he had been suffering from reverse culture shock and major depression because he had to come back to school instead of staying in Mexico, like he wanted. He had already been assigned to student teach that spring, and if he cancelled, it would be difficult to get another chance later.

He also shared that, despite the mission organization's rules, he had been dating a Mexican girl while down there.

Okay. I had an explanation. But it hurt almost as much as not knowing. His body ached for Mexico (or for the girl), and I could see it. As soon as he finished his teaching, he flew back to do a two-year stint there.

I think the worst part of any breakup is not knowing part or all of the reason. I'd spend countless hours retracing our times together or his words as he tried to explain. What does he mean behind the general statements: "It's not you, it's me," or "I don't want to lose you as a friend"?

Nathan—I can only remember one true breakup, and that was after a very short stint that never became very serious. For whatever reason, I broke it off with her right at Christmas before she went home for the holidays. How's that for sensitivity? I really didn't want that to happen, but I was so unhappy and didn't want to go through Christmas dreading her return. Sounds awful. She cried and cried. She wanted to be friends. Then, she would call me every week to sob about the fact that I hadn't called her to be her friend. Then I realized, we were broken up. I didn't have to answer for my infrequent phone calls; I was free. I finally said, "Listen, I thought we could be friends, but you are making me very uncomfortable." I know it hurt, but it was probably best, and she wasn't continually waiting for my call.

I've had a lot of dwindle-offs: dating situations that never got anywhere and eventually dwindled off with no hulla-baloo. There was the one girl who lived more than two hours away whom I'd drive to see. We would always have a blast. She always returned my calls, but I could go a full month without calling her, and it wouldn't bother her in the least. During our last conversation, she announced she was going to seminary in a couple of months when she finished her master's degree. I wished her well and said we'd talk later . . . but we never did.

Other Voices

Heather Floyd, Point of Grace—*It bothers me when a married person says, "I know how you feel." It's the most noncomforting thing to say. They don't know me that well. I'm a totally different person from them. I'm being affected differently from them. Maybe it would be better to not say anything but instead just give a firm hug. We don't need advice or some kind of wisdom. My mind is on what I'm going through. I'm not going to hear the words anyway, probably, but I can always feel a hug, and I can always hear "I love you" or "I'll be there for you."*

Someone who is married, even if they've been single most of their life, no longer knows how you feel. They're not there anymore.

I do know that God knows how I feel. He created me the way that I am and He can say, "I know exactly how you feel. I put those feelings there. You are responding the way I knew you would." That is very comforting to me. I don't have to explain it to Him. He already knows.

Recovering from a Broken Relationship
"There are plenty of fish in the sea."

Lana—Christian counseling can be very helpful in dealing with rejection. I think we are the most motivated to improve ourselves when we've been rejected. We wonder, *What's wrong with me?* Through counseling, we can learn better ways to communicate, work on our issues, and get a fresh perspective. One thing that I learned through counseling is to express and recognize my feelings. I had to unlearn stuffing them. I also learned to recognize some of the lies of the world. I had based a lot of my self-worth on my performance. The book *Search for Significance* was very helpful in recognizing these lies and how much God really loves me.

I also recommend doing things that allow you to feel good about yourself. Spend time with friends. Go and have a massage. Take a trip. However, don't get too busy that you don't take time to feel. Feeling sad is necessary. If we stuff our feelings, they'll come out in other ways.

Dana—I can think of a million other things I would rather do than recover from a relationship. Relationships never end at a good time, and memories of companionship, whether the relationship was healthy or not, seem to linger on far too long. When a relationship ends, I need time, not well-intended words. I need time to feel whatever way I am feeling and time to heal. If I feel like crying one minute and watching TV the next minute, that needs to be okay. I need to get past the initial breakup phase so I can begin to heal.

I wish I could bounce back after a relationship ends like a lot of guys do (or at least are able to make others think they do) and move on quickly. But I am wired differently. Even though I may know the relationship was wrong, or even if my feelings really

weren't deeply invested in the guy, I just think I am more emotional. And breakups are always worse on the receiving end.
After the shock wears off, the loneliness sets in, and then I
often go through the "I don't need you anyway" phase when I
really need to check my attitude. Instead, I need to try to look at
the whole situation through God's eyes.

A friend said that a positive way of looking at a relationship's
end is to see that "God is just shuffling." If He truly has someone
in mind, that person will be the right person. I would try to
encourage a person to recover from a relationship in that way,
trusting the Lord to have His control of the situation. It's so hard
to do, so much easier to say than to live out, but I have held on
to His promises to love and care for us and never leave us. It is
so much easier to work through any painful situation knowing
that the Lord's plans have consistently been better for me than
mine. And I have found contentment in my singleness when
I've told myself that I don't want a relationship or a situation to
happen if God doesn't want it for me.

Nathan—I haven't had to recover for more than a day or two. I
would have regrets; I would feel bad about my situation or
myself, but I would eventually develop the attitude that I was
better off and in control of my happiness when I was alone. I
think we must learn to be happy alone because we aren't guar-
anteed anything else.

If someone were trying to recover from a broken relationship,
I don't know what I would tell him, having not really gone
through it myself. The only thing I can think of is mourn. You
have lost someone, you have lost part of yourself, you have lost
a particular life to which you were accustomed. So I think you
must mourn. Then, you will be able to go on. But I think you
should take time off from dating and work on yourself and heal.
That's all I can think to say. Don't let friends or family cut your

mourning short, but expect yourself to pull together and accept that it is over. One friend told me, "I just had to look in the mirror and say, 'He doesn't love you anymore,' before I could really start to mourn and then to heal."

It's sad, but life is temporary. We will be home one day.

Chris—I just don't have much compassion for someone in this arena, especially for my high school students. I feel like relationships start and end, and we move on. It is just part of the process. It seems that anything you say would sound like a pat answer to them anyway. "There are plenty of fish in the sea." "You'll be better off without him." "Boys are scum." "I didn't like him anyway." "You're only fifteen; why the tears? Wait till this happens when you're thirty."

The best remedy to breaking up is to start dating again. I don't mean fly off the rebound on your way home from the "we-gotta-talk" talk. Donate a little time to rehashing every conversation, replaying everything you did right and everything you did wrong, and crying over the loss. Then get out there and find someone else. Once you let yourself fall "in like" again, your thoughts may be consumed with someone other than "him."

According to Joshua Harris in his book *I Kissed Dating Goodbye*, dating is not preparation for marriage like it seems. He proposes that dating is preparation for divorce. We can get used to breaking up, especially when things get a little tough.

Other Voices

Gary Mullet—*When you break up with somebody after being with them for a while, then it is like, "Good grief, I'm almost thirty. Now I've got to start all over again." So it kind of stinks. So I have not really been dating all that much. When you're serious with someone, you're not really dating anymore. Then when you break up, suddenly you are back at square one.*

Max Hsu, Church of Rhythm—I'm the wrong person to ask about that. I'm the wounded puppy guy. It took me eight months before I was over my last relationship. A friend recently said that as long as I was going to sit around and mope, it will hinder my ability to be used by God and that God really wants us to get ourselves together and move on. I don't move on quickly or well. I'm just one of those guys who sits around and mopes forever, still hoping the phone will ring months and months down the road. I'm still in that "everything reminds me of her" phase.

It takes me about as long as the relationship was to get over it entirely. But I think that is kind of good. I don't think I want to lose that about me. I don't want to be one of those people who's like, "Okay, well, that was dumb," and I'm dating someone else two weeks later.

Grover Levy—Just hang in there. I think those things just go in cycles. I think you've got to be willing to experience the full pain of the breakup and not just brush it aside. If it was somebody you cared about and it ended, let yourself feel the full extent of that pain, and then if you do that and you work through it, in time that pain will go away. I think you'll be a stronger person for it and you will realize, "Well, it's a good thing that it didn't work out because now I'm seeing that it wasn't what God intended." We have to trust that God knows what is best. We can't always tell that in the short term.

Rebecca St. James—Direct all that extra attention that you gave to that person and that time and that energy and that focus just totally on God. Where you may have gone out with that person on a Friday or Saturday night, spend it with God. Go for a walk. And just grow that best friendship with God and that focus on Him. We can never go wrong when we are growing our relationship with God. It's something that makes us more whole as people.

If you're searching for that human element, go out with some Christian friends in a group atmosphere where you don't have to worry about: "Is that person interested in me?"—just Christian fellowship because we massively need that too.

Michael Passons, Avalon—Don't expect them to come back. You can waste a big chunk of life waiting, thinking any day that they're gonna call. It would be great, if it worked out, but chances are it won't. I've wasted a lot of time. It's a good time of evaluation of who you are, your self-worth, and your worth in God.

Cherie Paliotta, Avalon—Getting over a ten-year relationship was probably the most painful experience of my life. I have learned from trial and error that the only thing you can do when your heart is so crushed and you are so depressed and hurt is to saturate yourself with the Word of God and pray and fast and seek Him morning, noon, and night. And you need to saturate yourself with godly fellowship, with people who love you and care about you. God is not going to let you go through that alone. I am living proof that God turned it [the pain from the ended relationship] all around for His glory and the situation is being thrown right back in the Enemy's face. People are getting touched and healed and delivered from pain by hearing of my experience, the very thing that the Enemy wanted to attack me with.

Dr. John Trent, Encouraging Words—I'm real big on encouraging people that they simply cannot out-logic emotions. If I were to step on your foot right now, instantly you would have a reaction and it would probably be an emotional one, "Ouch" or even anger. Then you can say, "John's kind of clumsy. He's being apologetic and my foot is getting better. So it was just an accident." Well, what came first? The emotion. If the goal of a single person is never to feel an emotional negative about being single, it will never happen. It's like Martin Luther said, "You can't keep birds from flying over your head, but you can keep them from building nests in your hair."

Look for fulfillment in relationships, with Christ first and then with others. You'll never find it in isolation. Some people will say, "I don't want to go to a singles' group." Why not? Then go to some other group. The point is to get into a group of friends, because isolation isn't really life.

Nee-C Walls, Anointed—When I was down people would tell me, "Honey, seek the Lord, seek the Lord. He's gonna hook you up. He's gonna bless you with that man." I got to the point where I was sick of that. I felt like I was seeking the Lord. I've learned that I need to give Him more control, and I have come to grips and confessed, "Lord, forgive me for even trying to get by without You. You created me. You know everything about this product that You created."

Pam Thum—Don't jump into another relationship. You've got time. Allow yourself time to heal. Keep running to God. Once a week do something for somebody else who is hurting in a similar way that you are. Then write down where your relationship went wrong, ask questions of God, and expect God, over a period of months, to answer those questions.

5

You Can't Waller in It
(Contentment)

This is our most "woe is me" chapter. We'd love to be upbeat all the time when it comes to being single, but that's just not honest.

We all know deep down inside that God has a plan. That plan is for us to be single today. Today is usually not the problem. But as today turns into years, we start questioning that plan. Doesn't He know how hard it is to be single? Has He not heard about the biological clock? Couldn't He just tell us if we will be single for life, instead of making us guess?

Our hope is that you will remember this chapter right after your ten-year class reunion where forty-seven people have asked, "Why aren't you married?" You can pick this up and realize that most single adults struggle at times with their singleness.

Becoming Content
"He wants me single right now."

Nathan—I hope I will never put off things because of the Impending Maybe.

So, we're single: incomplete, waiting, dissatisfied, lonely, half-baked. This is the way it seems to us and frequently to others. But I think that in the past, when society was faced with single people, it solved the "problem" in its own way. Marriages were arranged. Today, the approach is a lot more subjective. We have to feel sparks first before we commit. The price of such freedom can mean a significant amount of time alone.

Throughout this book, we've been dealing with the true wholeness of a single person in relationship with God. God is ever-present and ever-working. We must join Him. Waiting for the Impending Maybe of marriage is wasting the precious time that He has given us.

"Press on," says Paul in Philippians 3:12. How about charge on? Putting it off is a sin that could mean missing good things God has for me. I do not know what tomorrow holds. I can only base my knowledge on today. And today, it's just God and me. Tomorrow may be the same. If I am waiting for the Impending Maybe, what will I do at age seventy if I find out it was always the Inevitable Never? I will probably have missed the only important thing for which God put me here: participation in the historic flow of His perfect will. I am His before I am ever anyone else's. Being His is all I will ever need. It is hard: the moments can tick loudly in my ears if my main occupation is counting them. I want to be involved in God's will instead of wishing my time away.

I sometimes try to get away for a while during the day to read the Bible, study, and pray. I need this time to calm down about work stresses and reflect on the Lord of my life. It's stopping in the middle of the madness to take a God-filled breath. Living in the center of His will is where I've got to be. I'm learning to be in prayer always. I admit I get confused about it: how to pray fervently without sounding like a skipping, crackling record. By praying fervently, I will learn the voice of God. I believe that if I can get into the center of His will, I'll be not just happy but at peace and full of joy.

I think we all have the state of mind that we're in a holding pattern while trying to live as if we're not—putting on a good face. You know how you know something in your head and believe something else in your heart? I have to know that I am in a holding tank. God may very well have someone out there for me, and I should be in a time of preparation. At the same time, I need to believe that God and I are going it alone.

I am a single individual standing with God and making a life. It's God and me. How much better can that be? I pray that my contentment will be found in Him—that I will be enthusiastic about the life He is creating in me. I pray that this enthusiasm will spill over to others and that they will see Him in me. There can be uncertainty out there about tomorrow, but my constant prayer is that there will be excitement instead, that I can listen to His plan without interruption and be filled with strength.

Chris—I am so glad that I'm single right now. I am being used by God in ways I know I couldn't be if I were married. At least at this point in my life, I like not having to seek spousal agreement to do what I sense is God's leading.

As newspaper and yearbook advisor, I spend countless days after school talking to kids about their lives, their love interests, and their problems. I joke that my day doesn't even start till after school. The job I love would be so much more difficult if I had to run home to make dinner. My ministry would be affected if my attention were divided.

For example, I cosponsor Campus Life, a Christian club for teens. My coleader, Kent, is married and has three children. He has a sense of solidness that gives stability to the group. He always knows the right things to say and the correct ways to handle various situations, while I'm a little scatterbrained at times. He helps me focus on the important tasks instead of worrying about the minute details.

But I get to spend more time with the kids. He's got a full

plate at home, especially now that he's pursuing his master's degree. He's there for us whenever he can be, and I've come to trust in that, but even he admits that he misses out on some of that one-on-one time that builds relationships and brings on changes in the students we work with.

It has been two years since we restarted a chapter at the school, and more than once we thought of ending our attempts. But we are now starting to see that God has been working.

Recently, a sophomore girl asked if I could talk with her after school. The only place we could find to be alone was the restroom, so she inverted a trash can and sat as I leaned up against the wall. She openly said that she wanted to get to know God better and wanted to know how to start. After a few minutes of talking and praying (in the bathroom!), we left laughing. She has been reading the Bible and using the study guides I gave her. She's excited about the Bible study we're starting that will go through the summer. She's an open vessel, a sponge. Having a part in her growth has been one of the highlights of my year. Another highlight happened just days later.

We took the leadership kids camping. Because of his three small children, Kent couldn't commit to staying two nights at the primitive site. But I was able to stay with the eight kids and had a great time being one of them, playing euchre, melting bugs in the candle wax, and laughing at the guys cooking breakfast over an open fire. I was myself. I was relaxed.

The last evening we asked them to spend some time with God alone, then we came back together and recapped how God had worked through this school year. We were all crying and hugging each other as we shared the big and little things God had shown us. Devon, a sophomore football player, didn't share until the end. He seemed quieter than usual. He took a deep breath and started. "God and me are a lot like this caterpillar."

I hadn't noticed that he had been staring at a critter in his hand the whole time.

"At first, when I picked it up, it balled up and was scared. Then, little by little, it loosened up to where it is now—comfortable." It crawled to the end of his palm, then he inverted his hand to let it continue its path. In the dim firelight, I could see the tear or two he allowed to escape with his few words that summed up what Campus Life and God had meant to him.

That evening reconfirmed our commitment to these kids. We were making a difference!

By Monday, most of the school knew about our camping trip and especially how we shared on Saturday night. More and more we are getting a reputation as a place students can be real and be accepted.

It is so great that God chooses to use us, though He doesn't need to. He's given me skills and love and passion. Right now, He's given me the gift of time.

Lana—"Being content as a single" rings like an oxymoron to me. I think I am happy with life in general. However, I definitely want to get married and have a family, and I want to be able to love someone intimately. Does that mean that I am not content? Most times, I think I am, but I go in cycles. I think that is natural. Ever since I was a child I played house and imagined being married.

An individual struggling with singleness is similar to a couple dealing with infertility. We are both waiting on God, and the wait can be hard. We get our hopes up and then are disappointed. Those struggling with infertility go through medical tests, wondering what's wrong with them. If they choose adoption as an option, there's the screening by the agency, the meeting of the birth mother, and the praying that the birth mother would choose them. They barter with God for Him to provide.

It's similar to being single. The difference, however, is seen in the attitude of the church. The elders of our church will pray over, lay hands on, and anoint with oil a couple who is infertile. No one offers a "Be Content" seminar for sufferers of infertility. But singles are told to be content. When a couple goes to adopt a child, they don't usually have to worry about being rejected by the child. Sometimes I wish I could go to an agency to pick my mate. An agency could come to my house, have me complete a form, and match me with my mate, and I wouldn't have to worry that he might reject me.

When people think about how to treat singles, it's tricky. I admit that I don't want anyone to pity me or treat me as incomplete. However, I do want them to understand that I sometimes struggle with being single and would love their prayers. I can be generally satisfied with life but not happy with my marital status.

I generally consider that I have good self-esteem. The older I get, though, the more I start questioning: *What's wrong with me?* A friend of mine commented that when she asks herself that question, it concerns her external appearance. She thinks losing weight might afford her a better chance of meeting the right guy. For me, I focus on the internals: Am I too assertive? Too independent? Too direct? Since high school, I have tended to be a leader in various areas. I founded a Christian concert ministry in college, owned a company, and served in various leadership positions at our church. Is leadership a turnoff for guys? But I want to be who God created me to be.

I know I am called to be content in my circumstances. I want to be. No one is attracted to a bitter, negative person or someone who appears desperate. Even from a total marketing perspective, if I want to attract that special someone, then I can't be bitter or complaining. I often hear that if you are unhappy as a single person, you will probably be unhappy as a married person. Of the four of us who are writing this book, I seem to be the most anxious about my singleness, and I think it is because I am the oldest. I worry that I will never get married. However, I need to focus on the positive and take advantage of the situation in which God has placed me. I realize that lately I have put off things I want to do until I get married. I've decided not to wait any longer. Last year I traveled to Australia for three weeks. I went to Europe this year and am now saving to buy a house. I want to live my life to its fullest. As G. K. Chesterton said, "True contentment is a thing as active as agriculture. It is the power of getting out of any situation all that there is in it. It is arduous and it is rare."

Comparison is a weapon of the devil for creating discontent. I am very selective with whom I compare myself and to what circumstances. I don't tend to compare myself to the homeless or those in despair and thank God for His blessings. Instead, I tend to compare myself with the perfect couple at our church who has two kids, the dog, the great house, and two BMWs. And I'm not comparing their real life; I'm comparing what I perceive as their life. I need to remind myself that marriage can't be that easy and wonderful or so many would not get divorced.

Our singles minister once talked about writing his own book on singleness and was going to call it *Flies on a Back Door Screen.* Just like there are flies on the outside trying to get in, there are flies on the inside trying to get out. Today, many singles want to get married, while many marrieds want to be single again. It's a matter of perspective. We should make the most out of where God has placed us and realize there are advantages and disadvantages to both.

The best thing I can do to be content is remind myself that God created me and knows me best. True happiness is in the center of His will. I need to seek His kingdom continually and let Him take care of the rest. He will take care of my needs. Right now, that means I have this time to concentrate on His Word and my relationship with Him. A consistent quiet time has been hard enough. If I were married, I would have even less energy and time to get close to God because I would be striving to please my husband. That's why Paul recommended staying single:

> I would like you to be free from concern. An unmarried man is concerned about the Lord's affairs—how he can please the Lord. But a married man is concerned about the affairs of this world—how he can please his wife—and his interests are divided. An unmarried woman or virgin is concerned about the Lord's affairs: Her aim is to be devoted to the Lord in both body and spirit. But a married woman is concerned about the affairs of this world—how she can please her husband. I am saying this for your own good, not to restrict you, but that you may live in a right way in undivided devotion to the Lord. (1 Corinthians 7:32–35)

I still want to get married, but I want to make the best out of the situation I'm in.

Dana—It's often a real challenge even to think about being content in my singleness. It doesn't always make me so comfortable, but when has God ever wanted me to be comfortable? Too comfortable to look outside of my familiar surroundings and mind-set to see what He really has for me? He probably has not. I know God wants us to be moldable and shapeable, not stagnant and unchanged.

But God didn't say life would come without obstacles or temptations. At these times I am reminded of the passage in Habakkuk: "Though the fig tree does not bud and there are no grapes on the vines, though the olive crop fails and the fields produce no food, though there are no sheep in the pen and no cattle in the stalls, yet I will rejoice in the LORD, I will be joyful in God my Savior" (3:17–18).

So the Lord wants me to rejoice in the painful moments, in the seasons that seemingly will never pass, and realize contentment in all circumstances? Content with no clear career path, content in my nondating status, content in my gradually growing knowledge of the Scriptures? Wow! I must have been born of the fast-food industry mentality: I want everything, and I want it now—experience, knowledge, and wisdom—without enduring too many negative repercussions from my human choices.

Fortunately, God's grace extends to the stubborn, wandering sheep that I am, wanting to test the waters first and to trust in Him second. I am so convicted as I come to Him in prayer. I need to give the Lord some credit here. He knows of my desire to learn and grow in accordance to His will and wants to be there for me. I need to learn to receive that grace. I am so aware of the power of prayer these days as I learn what it means to pray without ceasing. He is helping me put my life in perspective, and I'm realizing how I can't function without Him. In my seeking to know and understand Him, the Lord is showering me with that peace and contentment that only He can bring.

Other Voices

Heather Floyd, Point of Grace—I'm not bitter about where I am. For some reason in His plan for my life, in His will, He wants me single right now. I could be discouraged or I can say that God wants to spend more time with me. He doesn't want me to divide my time with anybody else yet. He wants me to be His Heather and no one else's. And that makes me feel very, very special. He wants me all to His own right now.

Janna Potter, Avalon—It might sound bad: I like not having to be accountable, like when I go out with my friends at night. I have friends who are married and have to call their husbands or be home at a certain time. Not that we are doing something bad, maybe we go to a movie and we want to go to eat at 2:00 in the morning. The other thing is the money is mine to spend. The idea of getting someone else's opinion before spending money is an aspect I don't like. My mom said, "Marriage is great, and I love your father, but you have to understand, if you get married, there's another person to take into account." I am not ready yet. I can spend my money any way I want. If I want to blow it on something stupid, it's my choice.

Max Hsu, Church of Rhythm—I just came out of a relationship. What God said to me at some point—and I wasn't really happy with Him about it—was, "I need you to let her go so I can hold you more closely."

In the last five or six years, I've been dating nonstop. Different people, but long-term, committed relationships. Until this last year. After the last one God was like, "Okay, I need you not to date for at least a year." And I was like, "Sure," like I agreed in principle. "Sure, until I meet someone." But because I agreed to it, God kept His promise to me even if I wasn't gonna keep my promise to Him. So I've been not dating. For eight months God was like, "I'm not introducing you to anyone whatsoever." I swear I lived in a monastery. But in that time, I learned so much about God. I used to have a very "head" relationship with God, and I used to get my emotional needs met in a relationship. I would talk to God about the big things, but if I was upset or lonely, I would call whomever I was dating. What not dating has taught me is that there is a side to God that is very nurturing and compassion-

ate. And you can go to God for that. And there is a security
God can give you.

Cherie Paliotta, Avalon—The biggest advantage of being single is
there is no other person on this earth whom you can totally 100
percent put your trust in except Christ, and it causes you to lean
so much on Him for every single little detail. Being single and
being alone is just forcing me to get on my knees and say, "God,
please come through." Whereas if I were married, I might come
home and rely on my husband, and he's not going to be able to
fulfill every single need that God can fulfill.

Jaci Velasquez—Not having to report to anybody and being able
to say that "I did this before a certain age, or I did this before I
got married" is a great feeling.

Rich Mullins—God doesn't have to be good to anybody. He
doesn't owe us the breath we breathe. I figure if God has given
us salvation, that's way more than we deserve, and I won't
judge Him for not giving me something else.

Nikki Hassman—Being single is an advantage because I can
discover things about myself more easily, such as what makes
me happy, what doesn't make me so happy. I'm able to go out
to eat with friends or spend time alone to think and reflect. I
don't have to worry about sharing the bills. Independence—I
enjoy it.

Nee-C Walls, Anointed—I think the advantage is that I have
more time to spend with the Lord—to give Him more of me ver-
sus what a married person can because that married person has
her husband and things of the world to worry about.

Rich Vincent, Singles Minister—I am very honest about marriage. I'll say, "It's not as good as you think it is." I counsel women who are married who are lonelier than I've ever seen among singles. Not only are they lonely, but they are trapped because they are in this marriage that's not going too well. They don't communicate, and suddenly they are lonely; they can't move; they've got these children; there's no freedom. They're absolutely trapped and caged in this loneliness. The nice thing is, as a single, you have more freedom to do something about it than a married person has.

Cherie Paliotta, Avalon—Contentment has to be in Him and not in finding the right guy. It's like golfing. You can't get that ball in that stinkin' hole! You keep tryin' and tryin' and tryin' and the wind blows it past. It's the most annoying thing. That is what searching for a husband is like. There is no sense to it.

Heather Floyd, Point of Grace—Time is a huge advantage [of being single]. Independence too. But that's a blessing and a curse. It's nice to be independent, but sometimes I'd like to be dependent on someone. We were talking about it at church today that as singles we have extra time for God. Paul said that it's a blessing that we have this gift of extra time to become intimate with Him and for Him to become the Lord of our lives.

Jody McBrayer, Avalon—You think, One more year and maybe this will be the year. Then the next year comes and you think, This was supposed to be the year, and it wasn't. But you know I don't waller in it. You can't waller in it.

Jo Ann Anderson, Singles Minister—Singles look at marriage as the golden door. They think they'll be so much happier in a marriage. It's gotta be better than being single. Satan's biggest stronghold is that many singles think they can't be content unless they're married. My entire single life I thought that once I stepped over to the other side, I'd finally have the sense of being content and having fulfillment. It didn't happen. I have a really wonderful husband and a great marriage. I have a lot of contentment. But would I say I'm totally content? I'm still not. Marriage wasn't the antidote for discontentment.

Opening the Gift of Singleness
"What if God wants me single for the rest of my life?"

Lana—The gift of singleness seems like another oxymoron. It's like someone saying they have the gift of poverty. God gives you the grace for the situation you are in, but who wants to stay in that state? Everyone knows both the single and the poor are lacking something. Elisabeth Elliot has said that if you're single, then you have the gift of singleness; if you're married, then you have the gift of marriage. Whatever season God has you in, then He'll give you the grace you need. I like her perspective rather than the view that the gift of singleness is forever. I'll gladly accept the gift of singleness for a season. I just wouldn't want it forever and certainly would want to know how to return it!

Nathan—I learned about this phrase only after attending a singles' group in Indianapolis. My understanding of spiritual gifts is that they edify the Body and add to our individual worship of Him. Examples that come to mind are tongues, service, and prophecy.

I don't see singlehood this way. Certainly, if we are in the stage of life where we are single, we should use this time, as we would any, to grow closer to God. It can certainly add to our worship and edify the Body, but I see this time as a period when

207

we need to seek extra strength and grace from Him. It is also a time to focus on Him before we focus on someone else.

When we marry, do we then have the gift of marriage? Singlehood isn't an innate attribute but a time in which we are set aside for a purpose. I see those who never marry in two ways: they either missed people who God intended them to marry, or they have been set aside by God for singlehood. Perhaps they made a choice in response to His will, or perhaps God never provided the opportunity to marry.

555 Singles Surveyed

Do You Have the "Gift" of Singleness?

Yes   33%
No   67%

99% of those surveyed expressed a desire to marry someday. They must believe in the temporary gift of singleness.

Chris—I hear many singles ask, "What if God wants me single for the rest of my life?" as if they'd like to know so they can be bitter for a while and then not worry about the dating scene anymore.

I'm not concerned with getting married, at least not yet, at twenty-nine. I do worry about being passed up, though, as if the race has begun. What if all of my friends get married? What if I'm left behind? Singleness is a gift that each day we need to open and enjoy.

Dana—James 1 reminds us that every good and perfect gift is from above. The longer I live, the more I see my singleness as a priceless treasure from Him. I absolutely think God intends for me to be right where I am today: serving, learning, and growing in Him. He wants me to be available for His work whatever my marital status may be. Who am I to doubt God? He knows exactly what He is doing. As I compare my life to what it might be if I were married, I can't help but notice the free- dom my singleness brings. I definitely enjoy being in con- trol of my own schedule. Don't get me wrong, I can see myself mak- ing a quick and painless adjustment if those wedding bells were to ring. But for now, I look forward to the tasks He has for me as a single Christian servant.

> I HAVE LEARNED THE SECRET OF BEING CONTENT IN ANY AND EVERY SITUATION.
> —PHILIPPIANS 4:12

I am often accused of being too busy, and that may sometimes be the case, but I like to look at my schedule as maximizing my serv- ing time. I am the type of person who is willing to drop every- thing for a friend who needs to chat or for spontaneous runs for ice cream. I think the key is praying for balance. We are no good to the Lord if we allow work and good deeds to overshadow our real need to commune with Him. The biggest thing is allowing ourselves to be open to His leading. He may be leading us to cul- tivate friendships, spread some light, share our faith. Whatever the case, I feel my singleness lends itself well to my accessibility. There is a time for everything and a season for every activity under heaven. My time to be single is now, and I plan on mak- ing the most of it in utilizing the gifts God has given me.

Other Voices

Benji Gaither, Benjamin—Gift of singleness? Nah. I don't have that one. I don't know a man alive who has that gift.

Max Hsu, Church of Rhythm—I'm pretty sure that I don't have that gift. Deep inside me there's an ache, a hunger, to be in a relationship and to be close to someone. God is really teaching me how to use that productively and to get those things from Him and to be completely satisfied in Him. And I've had to come to grips with going, "God, it may be Your will for me not to be married, and I have to love You just as much." I'd have to accept that as something more beautiful than what I have in mind for my little plan. And that's a hard thing to swallow.

Eventually, if it is in His plan, I'll get married someday. If not, I'm gonna get a dog and a motorcycle, and I figure that will do in the meantime.

Rich Vincent, Singles Minister—The gift of singleness seems to be just for a short time for some people. It seems like at some point everybody has it, unless they go right out and marry. It seems to me that the whole idea of gifts in general is that we're to do all things for the edification of the Body and that while you are single you ought to be a gift to your Body, to your church, to your people.

I want people to know that singleness is not by any means a second-rate experience. I want them to know that this is number one in God's eyes in the sense that God will use someone devoted as a single just as much, if not more, than He will someone who is married and who has to divide his concerns.

Rich Mullins—My take on single life is, for those people who are too weak to handle celibacy, God gives a spouse. People who are too weak to handle a spouse, God gives celibacy. I'm pretty comfortable, I wouldn't mind being married . . . but I also believe that if you're not happy where you are, you're not going to be happy anywhere.

Greg Long—All my married buddies encourage me to enjoy the option of just flying to the West Coast because I have this week off. I literally do that; I'll hop on the plane and go. They say, "Enjoy that, Greg, because once you hook up, it's a whole different ball game." There are advantages in both worlds, and we need to be content where we are. . . . "The grass is greener" mentality sets in if I'm not careful, but married people don't have some of the freedoms that I have. We really need to believe that our life is in Christ's

Advantages to Being Single

Remember when your parents would say, "When you grow up and have your own home, then you can do as you please and let the dog sit at the table, but while you're under my roof, it eats in the utility room"?

Most people list freedom and independence as an advantage to being single, but here are a few more advantages:

- The remote is in *your* control.
- Go ahead. Drink out of the carton.
- You can blow three hundred dollars on computer games and come home guilt-free.
- You can opt to spend the weekend showerless.
- Live with reckless abandon. Leave the seat up.
- You can have a Barry Manilow day, and no one will laugh.
- You can eat it and reseal it, until it turns green.
- You can try that new gazpacho recipe with extra onions.
- You can belch out loud without saying, "Excuse me."
- Matching up socks is such a drag—just buy new ones.
- A night on the town is half the price.
- No need for panic that the sports section might not get back to its rightful spot.
- Monday night football can remain a sacred tradition.
- Sky-dive; bungee jump; climb Mount Everest. Why not?
- No one complains if you fix ramen noodles four nights in a row.
- Doing your taxes is EZ.

hands and put our faith to the test. If we believe that, then let's settle down. Be content. He'll take care of it.

And to follow that, He's gonna have us so busy doing stuff for Him and helping people find the Lord and helping people period, we're not going to have time to worry about it. We are going to be just so thrilled that God is using us and then, boom, if He wants to put somebody there in our lives to help us out, fantastic.

Mitch McVicker—I don't feel that I'm called to be single, just like I don't feel called to be married. I'm called to love.

Jody McBrayer, Avalon—Everybody is different. I desire companionship. I think God has put someone there to fulfill those desires.

Michael Passons, Avalon—Some people are called to singleness, and I think that is noble and that the Lord will give them strength as well.

Joshua Harris, I Kissed Dating Goodbye—*Any season of singleness is a gift from God. He has created this season as an unparalleled opportunity for growth and service that we shouldn't take for granted or allow to slip by. . . . While we're single, dating not only keeps us from preparing for marriage, it can quite possibly rob us of the gift of singleness.*[1]

Rich Vincent, Singles Minister—Especially in the Old Testament when you encounter someone single, you are encountering an exception because in a Jewish mind-set to have a family was one of the greatest blessings you could ever have. And so, for example, when Jeremiah was forbidden from having a wife, it was a horrible curse on him. It's clear in the New Testament *that being single has distinct privileges and advantages just as marriage has privileges and advantages.*

Struggling with Loneliness
"Will it always be like this?"

Chris—Okay. So I haven't gotten dressed yet, and it's 4:00 in the afternoon. I just don't feel like it. No one is home to see or smell me anyway. The day has been totally unproductive. I crawled out of bed around 10:00, started a load of laundry, sorted through junk mail while eating my Honey Nut Cheerios, crawled back in bed, and stared at the ceiling for a few minutes. A couple of heavy sighs later, I'm on the couch in front of the TV.

I hug my pillow, cry through *Beaches*, then flip channels enough to make my thumb complain about the workout. The couch becomes my dwelling. I only leave its comfort long enough to raid the kitchen of Fritos and JuJu candy.

I fluff my pillow and put it behind my head, thinking about how cool it would be to share this couch with someone. I'd lean into his chest, and he'd wrap his arms around me.

It's starting to hit me—I'm lonely today. I'm in that "woe is me" mode, and sometimes I just want to bask in my sorrow for a while. Sure, there are things I could be doing. I could take the initiative and call some friends who are probably also in their pj's watching reruns of *Roseanne*. I could do that. Or I could just sit here. I think *Happy Days* is coming on next.

Most days I know that I have a choice to be lonely, but I'm finding out married people can be lonely too.

Sarah married a youth pastor and moved with him to Oklahoma. She had no friends or family close by, and on a budget, she couldn't hang on the phone long distance. Within months, the marriage started having troubles, but she couldn't talk about them to any of her new acquaintances at church. They respected her husband, yet he emotionally abused her. She couldn't expose him to his own church. The guy she married, who she thought would meet all her needs, failed her. When a friend from home visited her, Sarah so needed to get out everything she had been dealing with that they cried together for two days.

People are mistaken when they think that loneliness can only occur when they're alone. You can be alone and be very content. You can be with forty people or the one you want to be with forever, yet still have feelings of loneliness.

I feel the loneliest when I'm with a group of happy couples. I can remember last Fourth of July when I was with some singles watching the fireworks. In my view the entire time was a good friend with her boyfriend. I tried to shift my position, but if I wanted to see the fireworks, I had to watch them hold each other, whispering in each other's ears and laughing.

Surrounding our blanket were lots of couples and their families celebrating the day. Dad lighting sparklers for his little girl with big, brown eyes. Mom handing out the picnic goodies, wiping chocolate from the mouth of the over-anxious two-year-old who kept pulling away. Frisbees flying. People laughing.

I was consumed with loneliness. Through the "oohs" and "aahs" of the fireworks watchers, I sat there and thought. Just earlier, at dinner, my friend's boyfriend, who always seemed to be concerned with my datelessness, asked the weirdest quest-ion that was totally uncalled for: he asked why I thought I wasn't dating anyone. How am I supposed to answer that? Because I'm fat and ugly and no one likes me? Because I'm too dominating and I repel guys? Because I'm not one of those petite little things who giggles and tosses her hair as guys talk to her?

I didn't know how to answer him, but as I watched the fireworks through teary eyes, I thought about all the big and little things guys would find wrong with me. And, in the midst of thousands of people at the park, I was lonely.

Nathan—I once heard someone say in a sermon that loneliness is a gift. He explained that God sometimes places people in lonely times so that they can reach out to Him—so that they can make God their sole source of sustenance.

I have been wondering if God puts us into loneliness to teach us to reach out to Him. Sounds sort of Old Testament Job-like. I think loneliness is simply a circumstance that arises. I think that if I am lonely, I should realize it and turn it into "alone-with-God-time."

It makes me wonder if it is a sin to be lonely, if that means I am not reaching out to Him or am not wholly trusting Him with my future. I am trying to reach that perfect love relationship with God. I, in fact, believe that this process is the very reason for my being. Sometimes I drive out to a park to study and pray. This is the time that I am trying to set aside.

I also use mornings for reading and praying. It seems like a better time to get on my knees and ask God to consecrate the day.

I don't fret loneliness on a day-to-day basis. I realize that I seldom have a sense of being lonely in the moment. I know that some people in my family worry that I am lonely, but it frankly hasn't struck me. The idea of a life ahead devoid of intimacy is what causes me to fret. I pray that God will always remind me of what is to come: I will soon be in heaven where I will reside in the arms of my Father. Right now I must draw nigh to Him so that He will draw nigh to me.

How can we be truly lonely with the omnipotent, omniscient, omnipresent Creator of the cosmos as our companion?

I'm not sure if I can entirely believe that it is a sin to be lonely. I think that my sin separates me from the love of God, therefore I am susceptible to loneliness. I should ever be exhaling a prayer to my Lord to keep me from sin, for then I will be entering that perfect love relationship that is as unknowing of loneliness as the sea is of arid land.

Lana—The times I feel lonely are usually the days when I have nothing planned and wonder, *Doesn't anyone want to be with me?* I need people around. That's where I draw my energy. I need to share my life. I need to tell someone about my day and to ask how his or her day was. I need to connect with them emotionally.

Loneliness visits everyone, married or single. We all need affirmation that we are loved and valued. When I feel lonely, I try to spend time with those I know love me. It's not the time for me to try to meet new people. I often will go to visit my best friend and her family. Just spending time with them reassures me that I am loved.

I also try to recognize the times I feel the loneliest. It often relates to that monthly cycle when, like it or not, for no good reason, I get down. Or it could be those typical events, such as holidays, that bring me down. I try to be proactive and plan ahead. It's also important to me that I realize that my mental, physical, and emotional health are all related. If I don't have enough sleep or am eating junk, I am more prone to get depressed and feel alone.

Dana—It's a constant battle to believe that God is all I need when I'm lonely. How can I be content when I long for that special dating relationship, when I reach out and no one reaches back? Can God hold my hand and embrace me after a long day? Will it always be like this?

It takes time to discipline myself to seek God first before imperfect human relationships. I do know that God is with us wherever we are in our walk with Him, in our quest to understand our feelings and desires. God doesn't leave us physically alone when we are in need. He provides brothers and sisters to reach out to us and reciprocate that giving.

To work through my loneliness, I am learning that I have to be completely dependent on God. It is so natural for me to surround myself with friends and family who understand me and have been there. But I know if I get in a habit of depending on peers to bring peace, tackle my situations, or discern my feelings and emotions, I overlook God's reasoning and true understanding of the big, eternal picture.

I want the tangible things—the friends to give me a hug and tell me everything is going to be okay, and especially, a male companion who is concerned about my heart, my whereabouts, and my ability or inability to endure life's latest scenario. Having those tangible things makes sense until someone disappoints me or falls short of what have become my secret expectations. Imagine that! A human misses the boat, takes a neutral stance, or seems to lose some sensitivity, and my need for the Lord suddenly becomes very clear.

My friends' desire to be there for me is not the problem. I'm the one who loses focus. How can I expect to find joy in any situation without first going to God to receive peace? He knows me better than I know myself. His Word says He knows the desires of our hearts, the plans He has for us—but He wants us to trust in Him for fulfillment, for peace, and for His timing. He wants to be all we need. And I want Him to be my strength, my comforter, and my confidant. But I don't always know how to look up, stand tall, and walk boldly in Him.

I will never think it wrong to seek wise, godly counsel and encouragement from a caring friend, but the main purpose of this feedback should be to encourage one another in what God has for us.

I value my friendships now more than ever; I can't imagine what I would do without them. This has become even more apparent as I have been blindsided by the budding romances in the three-hundred-member singles' group I attend. I am very happy for the new couples, but the last thing I want is my friend's new interest to hinder the frequency and quality of our conversations.

I am learning that is the risk one takes in becoming friends with other singles . . . but I still worry about losing those treasured friendships.

In God's eyes, though, this "you stole my friend" situation is another little Dana trauma that I need not waste my time and energy worrying about. I need to rest in knowing that God will provide the necessary friendships and accountability at any given point of time in my life. I should be focusing on what God has for me now. God is perfect. He is never going to leave me alone, let me down, or dismiss my loneliness. He can take hold of me, calm my fears, and comfort my heart. I just have to be open to His desires and let Him. I guess I know what I need to do; it's just that "having faith and letting Him" part that I need to work on.

Other Voices

Michael Passons, Avalon—I think when people are struggling with singleness they are struggling with loneliness. They're trying to fill the void that has to be filled with God. We get so hung up satisfying our loneliness with other people that we forget our relationship with God. We perpetuate our loneliness by not getting ready for the next step.

Nee-C Walls, Anointed—I am going to have to deal with loneliness. I'm alone when I'm out on the road and around me are *other group members who are married. I have to sit and listen to them talk about their husbands and their wives. Then I come home, and it is just total quietness. It is a peace to a certain extent—I've learned to accept it as peace. If I look at it as loneliness, then the Enemy can blow that up. It can take over me and cause a lot of other things to come about because one thing attaches itself to the next. As long as I stay on my face before the Lord and continue to commune with Him and stay in His Word, He continues to comfort me in my singlehood. He really does. He lets me know that "I am already your man. I'm the One who provides for you. I'm the One who can comfort you. I'm your counselor. You can talk to Me whenever you want." He is the One who really knows me inside and out. As soon as I accepted that and accepted Him to take that position in my life—I was fine.*

Mark Lowry, Out of Control—*Everybody gets lonely. And there's nothing wrong with it.*

Jesus got lonely. Says so right in the book of Mark: "Jesus could no longer enter a town openly but stayed outside in lonely places." Because of the news of Christ's healing power He had to get away, become a recluse. He had to be alone. And the Bible calls where He went, "lonely places."

All of us have a lonely place inside our hearts. And being around other people, including our own families, can't change that. Some of the loneliest people I've ever seen are in America's cities. They're surrounded by millions of people, but they're walking around in their own private, personal lonely places.

The simple fact is this: We're not in Eden anymore. We've been kicked out. No one got to stay. Married, single, divorced, widowed, orphaned . . . everybody out. Evicted. And we've been lonely ever since.

Lonely for Eden.[2]

Greg Long—Honestly, I guess when I turned thirty it hit me a little bit. My dad got married when he was twenty-nine, and I had never worried about it in my life—and when I hit thirty I *thought,* I wonder if I should start thinking about tying the knot? *Then I thought,* When it's supposed to happen, it's supposed to happen. *Do you just know? How do you know? Everybody has their opinions on that, so I honestly think I just stay busy and really don't think about it that much. I really try to enjoy life. I don't know what God has done, except keep me busy—not that being busy is the answer, but being busy focusing on others and what God has for us.*

I think so much peace, contentment, happiness, and joy can be found in volunteering at a nursing home. Or asking, "What can I do in Nashville to help those who are less fortunate?" We think, How do I fill my spare time if I am not married? *There is plenty to do and plenty of joy to come from that. The Bible says that if we are faithful in the little things, He will give us bigger things to do. So as we are faithful in serving others, maybe God will find somebody whom He can trust us with as a mate.*

Geof Barkley—Don't be afraid of being single. It's not a disease. Learn to live with yourself. Be still and know that He is God. We forget how to be alone with ourselves and with God. Not that I have that mastered, but it is something for me to work on.

Nee-C Walls, Anointed—I kind of got tired of hanging out with single friends who just mope and are depressed about being single. Try not to dwell on it. The enemy can take that little bitty "I feel worthless," attach it to loneliness, and attach the loneliness to depression. It goes on and on forever, and he continues to tell you lies and continues to beat you down. That's why you have to stay before the Lord and pray every morning and *ask the Lord to lead and guide you and just help you in that area.*

Pam Thum—*I saw this drama, an Easter production in which Jesus is on the cross and talking to the two thieves. One thief turns to Him and says, "Please remember me today," and Jesus says, "Today you'll be with Me in Paradise." Basically, the thief repented. It really hit me like it never had before, and I almost started crying. It was right after I signed a contract and was so busy—like eight times overseas in nine months. Jesus was dying for the world but He cared for the individual. In His last breath He could have turned and said, "Excuse Me. I'm in pain here. Just get in line with everyone else. I'm dying for the whole world, and you're a part of that." Reach out of yourself. The Bible says that if you refresh others, you will be refreshed.*

The Waiting Room
"God's timing is perfect; just be patient."

Nathan—It's nearly impossible, I think, to sit and wait. Doing something while you wait is, well, more *doable*. It's like being at an amusement park with your friends. Even though it's a drag to wait an hour and a half for a ride on the tallest wooden roller coaster in the country, at least you are there with them, talking and baking in the August heat together. Imagine what it would be like if you were there alone. You probably wouldn't be; it doesn't make sense.

That's why I shouldn't be alone and inactive during this time of waiting in my life. I should be handing out coats and gloves to the homeless, taking a glassblowing class at the Indianapolis Art Center, and participating in this writing group. It makes me realize life is more of a process and that I shouldn't be waiting for one big thing to happen to launch it.

Chris—"Be patient. God isn't finished with me yet."

The old T-shirt reminds me that every day I'm not with someone, I am being prepared. I'm not in a holding pattern. I'm not on standby. I'm in preparation.

Each failed relationship or each one I long for that never is to be, each time I sigh at the scale and think, "If I only lost ten pounds," each time I sit alone on a Friday evening, I'm learning something. I probably will look back on this time and know that this was my prep time—my time to figure out who I am, to understand my place in this world, to get things sorted out.

I didn't have any trouble having patience until I turned twenty-seven. I had already decided I didn't want to settle down until I had a good start on my life, and most of the solid marriages I had admired started when both people were twenty-seven. So I figured twenty-seven was a great age to marry. Then I turned twenty-seven and had no prospects. "You still have 364 days," my sister reminded me.

But suddenly, and for the first time, I realized that it wasn't going to happen in my time or on my deadline.

God sure taught me something. I'll be at this station in life until I'm ready to move to the next. Or maybe *I'm* ready, but this guy God's picked out for me is taking his sweet time in getting prepared.

Lana—When people tell me, "Just be patient. God has someone for you," I want to believe them, but that's not scriptural. God doesn't promise me that. He only promises to meet my needs.

Waiting is hard, especially when there isn't certainty. I have this image of waiting in the very long line at a ticket counter and the window never opens.

I am still trying to balance trusting God and making something happen. The old quote "Work as if everything depends on you; pray as if everything depends on God" seems fitting. I can trust God with my marital status, but if I never leave my house, it makes it a lot harder. Unless I want to marry a pizza delivery man or the UPS driver, I probably need to go out and meet people. I am active in a good Christian singles' group where I am expected to be seeking God more than seeking a date. I've joined a dating service and occasionally even have met men on the Internet. I try to be balanced in my approach. I don't want to be obsessed with dating.

I know that today it is God's will for me to be single. I can point to things in the past that I was able to do because I was single. Traveling to a foreign country or even writing this specific book are opportunities that may have not happened if I were married. I'm also glad that I have learned some of my hard lessons as a single, rather than stressing a marriage. God is indeed working all things for my good. It's the future that makes me nervous. However, God controls the future, and that gives me peace.

Dana—You know they say you should never pray for patience unless you really want to get it. Why didn't anyone warn me that my innocent, well-intended prayer would keep my patience lessons coming six years later? I keep thanking the Lord for His teaching in this area, all the while encouraging Him to move on to a different area of my life anytime soon.

The "God's timing is perfect" issue is not my favorite subject. This reminds me of the large-numbered watch that I wear on my wrist. "Hey, Dana, nice wall clock," my friends say. With all the hazing I'm getting, wouldn't it be great if one day my watch would encourage a second glance or comment from its ability to reveal God's timing? I could wear His watch and God would keep me in check with His way, saving me from much senseless doubt and worry.

Okay, so that's a bit far-fetched. I'm already feeling convicted in remembering what faith is all about. The truth is the Lord knows me well; He knows the areas that need bending and even breaking. I am a control freak. I want to plan everything—especially my future—and present my agenda to God so He can meet it. I have come to understand how crucial it is to observe where the Lord is already moving and adjust my actions to what He would have me do. I need to seek His perspective and work in obedience to accomplish His goals. He can fulfill us if we trust in His faithfulness, His exciting agenda, and yes, as we must, in His timing. Slowly and stubbornly I am learning that God's way is the best way—no matter how long or short the time frame and no matter how narrow the road to be taken.

555 Singles Surveyed

Top Ten Books Recommended in Alphabetical Order

1. Being Single in a Couple's World–*Xavier F. Amador and Judith Kiersky*
2. Finding the Love of Your Life–*Neil Clark Warren*
3. Fit to be Tied–*Bill Hybels*
4. God's Call to the Single Adult–*Michael Cavanaugh*
5. I Kissed Dating Goodbye–*Joshua Harris*
6. Lady in Waiting–*Debby Jones and Jackie Kendall*
7. Life on the Edge–*Dr. James Dobson*
8. Passion and Purity–*Elizabeth Elliott*
9. Quest for Love–*Elizabeth Elliott*
10. Single & Content–*Anders, Clement, Conti, and Trent*

Other Voices

Grover Levy—*I think it's okay to struggle. That's for sure. I struggle with singleness. I haven't always, but probably in the last couple of years I've wanted to be married. I guess you can't spend all your time focusing on that. You've got to keep your eyes focused on Jesus. Gosh, that sounds very cliché-ish, doesn't it? But it's also very practical. If you do that, then I think God will give you things to take your mind off of being single.*

Jaci Velasquez—Not everybody cool is married. Not everyone beautiful is married.

Rich Mullins—This whole "family values" thing is hugely misleading. It sort of implies that what your life is about is being happily married and having a beautiful family. And I go, "Wow, that's not what Jesus said."

You can have a wonderfully happy marriage or you can have a very successful experience with singleness and still not have anything at all when it's over. When we're dead, we're not married or single. And who we are is who we will be when we die. I think everyone should keep in mind that we will be dead very soon and live our lives in light of that. And your identity has to be something other than your marital status or your income.

Nee-C Walls, Anointed—Don't put yourself in situations that will cause you to want so much and long for it so much—like hanging out with married people all the time or hanging out with friends who are longing to have a man or a woman and just can't live without them. Desires aren't wrong—just pray that God will keep your emotions intact so you won't desire everything and everybody that comes along.

Rich Vincent, Singles Minister—Church people say some of the harshest, cruelest things from a pious mind-set when they give the advice to "seek first His kingdom and all these things will be added unto you." That is a very poor use of Scripture. I know a lot of singles whose desire of their heart is to get married and God hasn't provided, and now they've got to work on making sure that in their singleness they still learn how to be content, to love the Lord. They should make sure that the chief desire of their heart is to love the Lord with all their heart, soul, strength, and mind just like it should be any married person's or anyone's.

Dick Purnell, Single Life Resources—Some singles may feel like God has forgotten them. Somehow, He's given a mate to someone else younger or less mature or not as well-off financially. They think God doesn't like them. They probably won't say it but constantly beg or complain to God as if God were stingy.

"FOR I KNOW THE PLANS I HAVE FOR YOU," DECLARES THE LORD, "PLANS TO PROSPER YOU AND NOT TO HARM YOU, PLANS TO GIVE YOU HOPE AND A FUTURE."
—JEREMIAH 29:11

Heather Floyd, Point of Grace—When you're faithful to God, living a life He wants you to live, He really does give you the desires of your heart. Sometimes I fool myself into thinking my desires are different than what they are. The hard part is being faithful to Him all the time and making your heart pure all the time.

Rich Vincent, Singles Minister—Guys don't have a stigma if they're bachelors until their forties or fifties. But a woman starts gaining the stigma of an old maid. Why? You're not going to find that in the Scriptures. The pressures come on for two reasons: one, the social stigma and two, the biological clock. Whereas the guy just thinks, So what? I see a lot of guys and gals who are single by circumstance in the sense that they would like to marry, but God has not provided an opportunity. I also see some single by circumstance because they don't have that ability or confidence to approach people. I think that some people are single just for that reason alone.

Jo Ann Anderson, Singles Minister—Some singles have a couple of misunderstandings about God. First, some think, God has no idea of what it's like to be single. *It's so ludicrous. Jesus Christ* was single for thirty-three years. People just don't think about it. It's not how they relate to God. They don't relate to Christ as a single adult. It's almost never talked about. It's hardly ever brought up.

The second misunderstanding is thinking, God doesn't have a plan for my life or He's not watching out for me, because if He were, He would do something, specifically provide a spouse. *God loves us so much. He, as our Father, loves and cares so much. I try to help our singles remember how God was faithful in their past and help them realize that He still is and will be in their future.*

The Other Voices

Jo Ann Anderson serves as one of several singles ministers at Willow Creek Community Church in the western Chicago suburbs. Jo married when she was thirty-two and has one daughter. During our phone interview and our lunch together, we were encouraged by her heart for singles and felt truly ministered to.

Geof Barkley (mid thirties) played keyboards with Geoff Moore & The Distance until recently becoming a solo artist. After playing some concerts with Margaret Becker, Geof joined Geoff Moore & The Distance in 1988. In the 1996 CCM Readers' Awards, Geoff Moore & The Distance was voted third favorite pop group, and Geof was voted fourth favorite keyboardist. He said that his name is spelled Geoff, like Moore's, but he dropped the second "f" so he could be different. During the interview, we watched as Geof and Gary Mullet fought playfully about whose mom was better.

Larry Burkett is founder and president of Christian Financial Concepts, a ministry dedicated to teaching God's principles for financial management. His daily radio broadcasts are heard on more than a thousand outlets around the world, and more than two million copies of his books and workbooks are in print. Larry welcomed the opportunity to speak to singles about their finances.

Heather Floyd (late twenties) was born in Abilene, Texas, and started singing with Point of Grace in college. Point of Grace has won numerous Dove Awards and has enjoyed many radio hits. We interviewed Heather over dinner in Franklin,

Tennessee, where we especially enjoyed meeting and exchanging roommate stories with Heather's roommate.

Jeff Frankenstein (early twenties) lives in Nashville but grew up as a pastor's son in Michigan. Jeff plays keyboards for the Newsboys, who have a long list of Grammy and Dove Awards and nominations. A new homeowner, Jeff shares living space with a creative baker and with Geoff Moore & The Distance's Geof Barkley. We got a chance to talk with Jeff backstage at an all-day Christian rock concert in Illinois.

Benjamin Gaither (late twenties) is from Alexandria, Indiana. His group, Benjamin, has released two albums, As You Wish and Benjamin on Star Song. He got started early in music, since his parents are Bill and Gloria Gaither. We met with Benji in his parents' studio and found him to be a very laid-back fellow. We also got a demonstration of his new hobby: 3-D animation.

Joshua Harris (mid twenties) is a national speaker and the author of I Kissed Dating Goodbye. For four years he published and edited New Attitude, the Christian magazine for home-school teens. Harris lives with his wife, Shannon, in Gaithersburg, Maryland, where he is a pastoral intern at Covenant Life Church. He also leads New Attitude, a conference ministry with a mission of spreading a passion for God's truth and presence to young adults.

Nikki Hassman (early twenties) grew up in Waverly, Iowa, and sang with Avalon until signing as a solo artist with Sony Records in 1998. We first met Nikki relaxing in a hotel with her Avalon buddies, discussing "puffy-eye syndrome" and her quest for sleep during their demanding "My Utmost for His

Highest" tour. She also chatted about the close friendships formed among the four artists and her newfound ability to wear three-inch heels.

Max Hsu *(late twenties) was born in Hong Kong, where his parents are missionaries. He is one of the founding members of Church of Rhythm with Pamplin Music. He plays guitar, produces, and is in charge of "all things creative." Church of Rhythm snagged two Dove Awards for their song "Take Back the Beat." Max made the interview more like a conversation with a new friend because he asked almost as many questions as we did.*

Grover Levy *(early thirties) is a Nashville native who has recorded two albums on the Myrrh label. He became interested in music when he lived with a drummer and wanted his songs to relate to the spiritual seekers of Generation X. He didn't seem to mind having his dinner interrupted on a Sunday evening, and we chatted and ate together on the phone.*

Greg Long *(early thirties), a Myrrh artist from South Dakota, is no introvert and no stranger to music ministry. Greg now has three albums and has toured with many Christian artists. During our conversation, he caught our attention with his articulate, uninhibited responses and quick wit. His passion for music goes back to an early age. During his first solo of "Jesus Loves Me," at age three, he got scared and hid inside his dad's pulpit.*

Mark Lowry *(late thirties) comedian and singer with the Gaither Vocal Band, jokes about his singleness and many other aspects of life in his recent book* Out of Control. *We laughed so hard at the things he said; we just had to include some of his quotes. Always the funny guy, but with a great voice, Mark has touched the hearts and tickled the spirits of many.*

Jody McBrayer *(late twenties) is originally from Tampa, Florida, and now resides in Nashville. Jody sang with a performance group in college and then joined the band Truth. He now records and tours with Avalon on the Sparrow label. (Avalon won the 1998 Dove Award for the Best New Group.) We enjoyed seeing Jody's relaxed side, since he squeezed in a run before our interview and bopped in wearing shorts and running shoes.*

Mitch McVicker *(mid twenties) is most known as being Rich Mullins's sidekick. In* Canticle of the Plains, *a musical based on the life on St. Francis of Asisi and produced by Mullins, Mitch's vocals and writing are both featured. Making a tremendous recovery from the tragic car accident in September 1997 that took the life of his friend Rich Mullins, Mitch is now singing on his own and has released his first self-titled project on an independent label. We first met Mitch at a concert in our home church. Reserved with a quiet strength, we saw Mitch again, opening for Rebecca St. James, and were impressed that he remembered us.*

Michael Medved, *renowned movie critic and co-host of the PBS series* Sneak Previews, *is also known for his attack on society's images in his book* Hollywood vs. America. *Michael also sits in occasionally for Rush Limbaugh on his talk show. He objectively sees the impact movies and the media have on us and is rightly concerned. Michael and his wife live in California with their two daughters.*

Gary Mullet *(early thirties) is from Nappanee, Indiana, and is currently living in Shreveport, Louisiana. He played bass for Geoff Moore & The Distance. Geoff Moore & The Distance received the 1997 Dove Award for best long-form video (*Roadwork, *ForeFront Records). We talked to Gary right before* a youth concert at Anderson University in Indiana and discovered he's a person who enjoys shooting the breeze.

Rich Mullins, *former singer/songwriter with Myrrh records, lived on an Indian reservation in New Mexico until his tragic and untimely death in a car crash in September 1997. We talked with Rich on Super Bowl Sunday in 1997. Because we had mutual friends, we had seen him a few times. One night at our singles' group Rich and Mitch showed up in the back, and it was quickly announced that they would be doing a free concert after our meeting. Known as a person you really couldn't know, Rich was said to be a modern-day prophet. Rich was an honest person, even when you didn't really want an honest answer, and his lyrics focused on the eternal.*

Cherie Paliotta *(late twenties) is Avalon's new soprano. We couldn't help but admire her honesty and desire to seek the Lord first in everything. She has a noticeable northeastern (Johnston, Rhode Island) accent. Prior to joining Avalon, this Italian toured nationally with the praise and worship band Sold Out. She takes to all sports, especially horseback riding and skiing and, as a former music teacher, finds much joy in working with kids.*

Michael Passons *(early thirties) is a tenor from Yazoo City, Mississippi, who moved to Nashville after college. He traveled as a solo artist performing praise and worship music at conferences prior to joining Avalon. At the hotel we didn't recognize him with his ball cap until he introduced himself.*

Janna Potter *(late twenties) hails from Baltimore, Maryland, and now lives in Nashville. She toured with Truth before she co-founded Avalon with Jody McBrayer. When we met Janna in her* hotel lobby, she was in dire need of coffee, having traveled late the night before. Then she settled comfortably in a chair with a warm cup to talk to us.

Dick Purnell is founder and director of Single Life Resources. The author of twelve books, including his bestseller and award-winning Becoming a Friend and Lover, Dick has addressed more than a million singles. Single for forty-two years, Dick is now married and has two daughters. He welcomes singles to check out his web site at www.slr.org.

Dennis Rainey was involved in singles' ministries for ten years before founding the Family Life Today ministry. He says that after he covers any topic concerning singles the ministry's phone rings off the hook. He has authored several books, including The Tribute, in which he encourages adults to get right with their parents. Dennis appealed to us at the end of the interview to be honest in our writing. He understands that singles are hurting and challenged us to write as God would want.

Rebecca St. James (early twenties) is a native of Australia who now lives in Nashville. Her whole family travels with her as part of her concert and her ministry. Completing her third album, Rebecca was recently rated one of the top up-and-coming evangelists. We have enjoyed her two devotionals that are written with passion for her generation, and we used a few quotes in this book. Rebecca earnestly prayed for us before the interview and answered our questions with an honesty and a spiritual depth that shocked us because she was just barely out of her teen years.

The Other Voices

Pam Thum *(early thirties) is the only child of traveling evangelists and started singing at a young age. When she is not on the road, she divides her time between Grand Rapids and Nashville. She records on the Benson label and is a three-time Dove Award nominee. She was sweet and answered our questions over the phone in spite of a sore throat—even with a concert the very next day.*

Dr. John Trent *is president of Encouraging Words, a ministry committed to strengthening marriage and family relationships. Dr. Trent is a regular speaker at many conferences, including Promise Keepers, and has authored and coauthored more than a dozen award-winning, best-selling books. Raised by a single mom, Dr. Trent is married, has two daughters, and lives in Arizona. We met him at the Heritage Keepers conference and conducted the interview at his booth.*

Jaci Velasquez *(late teens), who admits she's not quite "single" yet, has already had a great impact on the Christian music industry with several top singles and two albums. Since first seeing Jaci in action, and now having spoken with her about her ministry, we were pleased to observe her spiritual maturity, her obedience to the Lord, and the desire to reach her peers for Christ. Jaci has received four Dove Award nominations and won Best New Artist in 1997.*

Rich Vincent *is the Singles Minister at College Park Baptist Church in Indianapolis. Each year he leads a seminar called "Navigating the Dating Maze" and is writing his own book on the topic. Rich can relate to singles, since he married at age twenty-nine and has only been married a few years. We found* him to be very approachable and someone who has a passion for knowing God's Word.

Denise "Nee-C" Walls *(late twenties), with her animated speech and unique vocal gestures, was so much fun to talk with. This powerhouse vocal talent moved to Nashville to join her friends, the brother and sister team of Steve Crawford and Da'dra Crawford Greathouse, to form Anointed. Nee-C also enjoys writing songs for the three-time, Dove Award–winning, Myrrh group. Anointed also received a Grammy nomination for Best Contemporary Soul Gospel Album.*

Mark Wesner *served as the Minister with Singles at East 91st Street Christian Church in Indianapolis for eleven years. East 91st is our church home, and we have enjoyed Mark's leadership and contributions to our singles' ministry. Mark and his wife Jenny have five daughters, ages six and under. He encourages singles to find their spiritual gifts and join God through service opportunities. In 1998, Mark shifted his ministry focus to small group ministries within our church.*

Survey Information

To better represent Christian singles in general, we surveyed 555 singles from four churches from around the country with large singles' ministries. More than 99% indicated that they were Christians. Thank you to the following participating churches:

East 91st Street Christian Church in Indianapolis, Indiana
First Baptist Church in Atlanta, Georgia
First Evangelical Free Church in Fullerton, California
Prestonwood Baptist Church in Dallas, Texas

Of the 472 who listed their gender, 43% were male and 57% were female. Of the 421 who shared their status, 81% were never married, 17% divorced, and 2% widowed. The age distribution of the 481 who gave their age was

13%	*18–23*
36%	*24–28*
30%	*29–35*
21%	*36+*

Notes

Chapter 1: From the Freezer to the Microwave in the Same Box
1. Mark Lowry, *Out of Control* (Dallas: Word Publishing, 1996), 116, 135.
2. Ibid., 122.
3. Ibid., 123.
4. Ibid,. 138.
5. Ibid., 196.

Chapter 2: God Gave All of Us Twenty-Four Hours in the Day
1. Mark Lowry, *Out of Control* (Dallas: Word Publishing, 1996), 136.

Chapter 3: Not Yet Promoted to the Grown-Up Table
1. Mark Lowry, *Out of Control* (Dallas: Word Publishing, 1996), 116.
2. Rebecca St. James, *40 Days with God* (Cincinnati: Standard Publishing, 1996), 94.
3. Ibid., 34.

Chapter 4: Looking for the Holy Grail Woman—or Man
1. Rebecca St. James, *40 Days with God* (Cincinnati: Standard Publishing, 1996), 56.

Chapter 5: You Can't Waller in It
1. Joshua Harris, *I Kissed Dating Goodbye* (Sisters, Oregon: Multnomah Books, 1997), 78.
2. Mark Lowry, *Out of Control* (Dallas: Word Publishing, 1996), 188.

The writing team of
Anders, Clement, Conti, and Trent

The four authors reside in Indianapolis and attend the same church. They developed the book's concept when, as writers for their singles' group newsletter, they saw that others might benefit from their stories, artist interviews, and pastoral challenges. For almost two years, they met weekly to develop that concept, pray for each other and for their future readers, and to munch Fritos.

Dana Anders (late twenties), the queen of the phone interview who milked the most out of the book's interviewees, currently serves as the worship coordinator for the single adult ministry at her church. She majored in both vocal music and journalism at Indiana University. Dana's love is ministering through music, and she is passionate about leading worship and singing in a local contemporary Christian vocal group.

Known for her Dana-isms, like calling something "Daner-friendly," Dana spends most of her time laughing and catching up with friends. She also enjoys traveling, swimming, writing, watching basketball and gymnastics, and attending big band concerts. She is often seen consuming large bowls of ice cream and is most content hanging out with family. With her love for Christian music and people, Dana especially enjoyed interviewing the artists.

Nathan Clement (early thirties), the big-word-of-the-week guy and token male, is a designer for a large publisher. He majored in his two favorite things, art and writing, at Indiana Wesleyan University in Marion, Indiana. Nathan designs books for computer users—you've probably used one— and chases down creative freelance work. He created the informational graphics for this book and designed the cover. He hopes to illustrate children's books someday soon.

When he was new to Indianapolis, Nathan sought out an active singles' ministry and attributes the one he found with helping him connect with new friends while receiving teaching from the Word. He realized there that singles form an undeniable community that somehow tends to remain on the outskirts. Together with his newfound friends, he set out to document, in roundtable style, the different life lived by unattached people.

Chris Conti (late twenties) brought years of writing and editing experience to the table, always ready with her trusty red pen. Chris earned a journalism degree from Indiana State University and is now in her seventh year of teaching high school journalism. She has a passion for working with youth and missions and enjoys annual trips to Mexico with teens to build houses for those less fortunate. She loves photography, writing, and desktop publishing, but expresses most of her creativity through teaching those subject areas.

Chris became a Christian as a junior in high school and grew in her faith during her college years with InterVarsity Christian Fellowship. An avid volleyball player, Chris also enjoys softball and swimming. The best part of writing this book, she says, was sharing her stories of humor and horror, and learning about the book writing and editing processes.

Lana Trent (mid thirties), rounded out the writing team, especially helping the group to stay focused on its task and to be prayerful about its ministry.

Lana, known for her humorous one-liners and for being an advocate for single-sensitive issues, is a Christian music buff who loves to travel. A computer consultant, Lana has an undergraduate degree from Purdue University in Communications and Psychology and a MBA from Indiana University. She has held several leadership positions within her church's single ministry as well as within the church. She presently leads a women's Bible study group and shares a house with one of her co-authors, Chris, and with Jodi, who Chris and Lana affectionately dubbed "Roommate Advisor" for the book.

Lana has been published in several publications and has spoken at various religious conventions/retreats on the topics of singleness and information systems. Serving as the writing group's business manager, she especially enjoyed using her marketing skills to analyze survey data and utilizing her knowledge of the Christian music industry to secure interviews.